D1014862

The Tactful Teacher

Effective Communication
with Parents,
Colleagues,
and Administrators

Yvonne Bender

Nomad Press

A division of Nomad Communications

10 9 8 7 6 5 4 3 2

Copyright © 2005 by Nomad Press

ISBN: 0-9749344-3-7

Questions regarding the ordering of this book should
be addressedto Independent Publishers Group

814 N. Franklin St.

Chicago, IL 60610

Nomad Press

2456 Christian St.

White River Junction, VT 05001

www.nomadpress.net

Also by Yvonne Bender:

The Power of Positive Teaching: 35 Successful Strategies for Active,
Enthusiastic Classroom Participation
and
The New Teacher's Handbook:
Practical Strategies & Techniques for Success in the Classroom

Acknowledgments

I wish to gratefully acknowledge the following people for their assistance in writing The Tactful Teacher*:*

Melanie Gaieski for many hours spent reading and reviewing, designing charts and forms, and offering advice on content and style.

Lauri Berkenkamp for editing that greatly improved the book.

Table of Contents

Introduction

As a beginning teacher many years ago, I was assigned a particularly challenging group of students. On my first day on the job, the assistant principal called me into his office and told me not to worry about student discipline problems: he strongly supported his teachers and if any students gave me a hard time, he would deal with them. I was new to teaching and determined to begin on the right foot. I spent long hours planning and preparing (what I believed to be) engaging lessons, but was unable to teach them because my students were so poorly behaved and uncooperative. After several futile attempts to get things under control on my own, I began sending the class troublemakers to my assistant principal, as he had told me I should, so he could deal with them.

Unfortunately, this strategy did not improve matters; rather, it made them worse. It wasn't long before the assistant principal called me into his office and asked me to stop sending so many students to him.

"Ms. Bender," he said. "I suggest you start building a more positive rapport with your students. I want you to meet daily with Mr. X and Ms. Y, who are veterans of this school, to get a few practical pointers on how classroom management is really done."

I did as directed, miserable that I had misunderstood my assistant principal's initial communication with me, and concerned that my teaching career was about to end before it actually began.

With the help and guidance of some kind colleagues, I made it through to the end of the year, and was even rewarded with a few, small teaching successes that inspired me to continue to a second year—and eventually a long and satisfying teaching career.

This rocky beginning forced me to quickly master basic classroom management techniques, but equally important, it made me acutely aware of the problems that result from confusing communication. After my unpleasant experience with the assistant principal, I was much more sensitive to all of the communications of others, and thus more attuned to the exact meaning of those exchanges.

As I gained experience in the work world, I learned that good communication builds good public relations—and good public relations are essential to successful teaching. Teachers with effective communication skills have more positive working relationships not only with their students, but also with parents, administrators, supervisors, resource personnel, and the community at large. More importantly, their highly effective communication skills help them resolve complex problems and avoid long-term difficulties that teachers with weaker communication skills often struggle to overcome.

When faced with angry parents, overly critical supervisors, autocratic administrators, less than helpful guidance counselors, or careless custodians, these tactful teachers employ strategies that keep the lines of communication open, the dialogue collegial, and help all concerned reach some measure of common agreement. They employ definite strategies to master the politics of difficult communication.

The Tactful Teacher contains many of these strategies and explains in detail how to implement them. These strategies are based on actual teaching experiences, and are explained in step-by-step detail. They provide effective, easily implemented solutions to vexing communication problems, and will help you communicate in a proactive, positive, and respectfully assertive fashion with those whose support and goodwill is essential to your teaching success—even when the information you must communicate is unpleasant and difficult.

Part I
Building Effective Communication

People communicate both directly and indirectly. Most direct communication is intentional and includes what we choose to say, write, and do. When we teachers distribute guidelines for a research paper, review them with our students, and insist that they follow them, we are using direct communication.

In addition to direct communication we also communicate in indirect and unintentional ways through body language, facial expressions, and speech patterns. Most indirect communication is the result of long habit, personality traits, and social customs. It is unintentional and requires a concerted effort to control. The beginning teacher who repeatedly asks "okay?" when working with her class unintentionally communicates her lack of self-assurance to her students, inadvertently inviting them to question her authority. In order to communicate in a more authoritative manner, she must become aware of that particular speech mannerism and consciously work to change it.

Communication is often complicated by our inability to accurately interpret how others are communicating to us. Did the speaker or writer really say what we thought he said, and mean what we thought he meant? If we misinterpret and respond inappropriately we may create serious (and sometimes long-lasting) difficulties for others and ourselves. The way to prevent such misunderstandings is to understand and implement effective communication strategies.

WHEN BODY LANGUAGE SPEAKS, SEE WHAT IT'S SAYING

Inadvertent behaviors can, depending on the circumstances, communicate useful information about the people exhibiting them. People who sit facing away from a speaker with their arms and legs tightly crossed are often revealing resentment, anger, or discomfort, especially if the speaker is relating unpleasant information to them. Those who hang back during introductions at a back-to-school night, rejecting handshakes and avoiding eye contact, may be revealing shyness, social ineptitude, or distrustfulness, while those who violate their listeners' personal space by standing within inches of them during a discussion about school policies are often revealing an in-your-face aggressiveness and belligerence. See the Appendix on page 131 for more information on interpreting non-verbal communication.

While all body language doesn't necessarily have hidden meanings (people sometimes yawn only because they're tired, not because they're bored, or glance at their watches only because they want to know the time, not because they're anxious for a meeting to end), some behaviors—when viewed within certain contexts—speak volumes about the people exhibiting them.

TEN STRATEGIES FOR BUILDING EFFECTIVE COMMUNICATION

The following are some strategies you can use to make your communication skills more effective.

1. Adjust your communication to fit the situation.

2. Know and follow your school's communication chain of command.

3. Open lines of communication before problems start and work to keep them open.

4. Begin positively.

5. Practice active listening.

6. Emphasize areas of agreement.

7. Be willing to compromise.

8. Respect confidentiality.

9. Avoid gossip.

10. End on a positive note.

1. Adjust Your Communication to Fit the Situation

Just as you modify your behavior to fit a setting and situation, you also modify the way you communicate to do the same. Your behavior and communication style, for example, are much different at an old friend's birthday party than they are at a faculty meeting. At a birthday party they are informal and casual, at a faculty meeting they are formal and professional. Since successful communication requires that you change your tone to fit specific situations, it is helpful to sharpen your awareness of both the effective and ineffective communication behaviors used by your co-workers.

Observe the people around you during their conversations with others and take note of the behavior of the various participants. Notice the language they use and when they choose to use it. Is it informal or formal? Is it filled with colloquialisms and slang? Does it contain a great deal of educational jargon? When and with whom is the language most formal?

Observe people's body language. Do they have their arms folded tightly in front of them? Are their hands on their hips? Are they standing within inches of the people with whom they are speaking or are they standing several feet away? Is the speaker standing and the people being spoken to seated or vice versa? Notice everyone's overall demeanor. Are there occasional nods of agreement and smiles of goodwill, minimal reactions and blank stares, or angry shakes of the head and scowls? What topics seem to cause the greatest reactions and from whom?

At the conversation's conclusion does everyone seem to be satisfied? If not, who seems to be the least happy? Is it the person who was perturbed when the conversation began or is it someone else? If the conversation involved several people, does the entire group disperse immediately upon its conclusion or do two or three people remain behind and continue to talk?

Observing behavior and answering these questions sharpens your awareness of the dynamics of communication. This aware-ness gives you information that can help you modify the way you communicate so you are more readily accepted and easily under-stood by your intended audience.

For example, your observations during an informal back-to-school night or parent–teacher meeting might lead you to conclude that:

• The parents at your school generally respond more positively when teachers communicate with them in straightforward, non-technical language; or conversely that the parents at your school generally respond more positively when teachers communicate with them using higher-level technical terms.

- Certain parents are much more at ease during a parent–teacher conference when the teacher sits together with them instead of remaining behind his desk throughout the meeting.

- Your administrator is more comfortable meeting with parents in her office than she is meeting with them in a classroom or vice versa.

- The body language of some parents, administrators, and teachers seems to consistently contradict their spoken language. For example, the "closed" body language of the administrator (standing at full height with his arms folded tightly across his chest) seemingly contradicts his comment to the small child, "In order to be fair about this, I'd like to hear your side of the story."

This information can aid you in making appropriate changes in your language choices, seating plans, meeting format, and demeanor by giving you insight about whether it's better to use technical or non-technical language when sharing information with parents, the most beneficial seating for a parent–teacher conference, the best place for parents to meet with an administrator, and the inconsistencies that might exist between your spoken and unspoken communication.

2. Know and Follow Your School's Communication Chain of Command

In almost every school system a healthy respect for the communication chain of command equals a long and administratively hassle-free teaching career. Learn your school's established way of communicating down the ranks as soon as possible when you begin teaching—it may be confusing in the short-term, but vital for your long-term success. The chain of communication command may mean something as simple as remembering to inform your school's administrator of your intended actions before informing parents of them, or requesting help from a school-based mentor before requesting help from outside sources.

You can learn about your school's chain of command through research and observation. If your school has a teacher's handbook, review the section describing job duties and responsibilities and take note of who has responsibility for what. Then be sure to inform that person before you take action in his or her area of responsibility.

For example, say you learn from reviewing your teacher's handbook that the assistant principal is in charge of end-of-school dismissal procedures. When a parent sends you a note requesting permission for his son to ride a different bus that afternoon because of a dentist's appointment, you should follow the appropriate chain of command and send the parent's note to your assistant principal, allowing her to act upon the request.

While it might seem easier and less time-consuming to simply handle the parent's request on your own, remember that a break-down in the chain of communication command often results in unfortunate consequences. For example: your assistant principal might well note the student is missing at the end of the day and incorrectly conclude that:

- The missing student is dilly-dallying around and is late coming to the bus (causing your administrator to hold up a bus full of impatient and noisy students while she finds out the missing student is on his way to the dentist).

- The student has left school without permission (causing your administrator to contact the bemused parent who then informs her that his son is at the dentist).

- The student was kidnapped by his non-custodial parent (causing your administrator to contact the less-than-amused parent who then informs her, after a quick phone call check, that his son is at the dentist and then questions your administrator's competence).

In all of these potential scenarios your assistant principal ends up feeling embarrassed or irritated—most likely at you.

In addition to reviewing the teacher's handbook, you can learn much about your school's communication chain of command from your colleagues. Ask them for advice about whom to contact with a concern and the best approach to use when doing so. Use your own best judgment: be somewhat skeptical when you receive advice that directly contradicts the information in your teacher's handbook. For example, cavalier advice from a colleague such as, "Don't worry if you can't get out on bus duty on time, there are plenty of teachers to cover for you" should be disregarded if it contradicts written administrative directives or faculty meeting statements by your principal that stress the importance of teachers reporting promptly for bus duty. Also, be aware that within the hierarchy of accountability, a written directive has considerably more weight than a spoken directive. If you get into trouble for disregarding a written directive (either through ignorance or willfulness), you cannot justify your actions by declaring others misinformed you.

LEARN YOUR SCHOOL'S CHAIN OF COMMAND

- Carefully review the job duties and responsibilities section of your teacher's handbook.
- Do not take on others' responsibilities without gaining their permission to do so.
- Seek guidance from experienced colleagues regarding whom to contact with a concern.
- Be wary of advice that seems to contradict your school's administrative policies.
- Read and follow through on all written directives.

DECIDING WHOSE ADVICE TO TAKE

It's easy finding people who want to give advice, but it's difficult knowing whose advice to take. First, you must take advice from those above you in your school's administrative hierarchy, since they are the ones in charge. Depending upon your school, this might include your principal and assistant principal(s), subject area supervisor, department chair, team leader, and administratively assigned mentor. Therefore, if you decide to seek advice from your administrators, be prepared to follow their suggestions even when you disagree with them.

You are not required to take advice from anyone other than those in the administrative hierarchy, but if highly respected colleagues offer advice, it's wise to consider it carefully. Since it's often difficult when you enter a new situation to know who among your colleagues is highly respected, take the time to determine who will be a valuable source of information and advice, and who will not.

Observe the dynamics that take place between the adults in your school. Notice those people who are highly respected by administrators and those who are highly respected by your teaching

3. Open Lines of Communication Before Problems Start and Work to Keep Them Open

Since it is difficult to discuss problems with people or request their help to resolve complicated issues when you have had little or no contact with them, it is important to open lines of communication before problems arise and work to keep them open. You can do this through emails, newsletters, notes, phone calls, formal conferences, and informal meetings. (See Part II for more on this topic.)

4. Begin Positively

Since people are generally more receptive and cooperative when they are approached in a courteous, non-threatening manner, begin colleagues. Take note of who is respected by both administrators and teachers and seek them out as your primary sources for judicious and helpful advice.

If it is unclear to you who is more highly regarded by the administration, seek advice from those who are most respected by your fellow staff members. For example, this might be a teacher who has taught at your school for many years and has worked with many different administrators, or a teacher who is always elected to the faculty council or as union rep because he or she is adept at voicing teachers' concerns. However, regardless of how much your colleagues respect this teacher, it's wise to view his or her advice with some degree of caution, especially if it does not seem to agree with your administration's preferred practices.

Reject all advice from colleagues who are frequently disgruntled and negative, even when their advice agrees perfectly with your own negative perspective at the time. For example, if the staff curmudgeon who always complains about having to attend after-school faculty meetings advises you to, "Stand up to the administration!" by joining her and her friends in their boycott of the next faculty meeting, you really probably shouldn't.

your communication with them as positively as possible. Starting positively is especially helpful when you know that a discussion will eventually cover some difficult and unpleasant topics.

First, regardless of how nervous or harried you may feel, always begin meetings by properly introducing everyone. If there are several participants who have not met before, distribute nametags or place name cards at each person's seat. These will help introduce people to each other.

After the introductions, make a few positive comments concerning the meeting's participants or the topic at hand. For example, a teacher who is meeting with parents to discuss their child's lack of reading progress might say, "Hello, I'm Mrs. Rose, Billy's reading teacher, and you must be Mr. and Mrs. Edwards. I'm so glad you could meet with me to discuss Billy's reading progress. You know, one thing I've noticed about Billy is that he's a hard worker who's determined to do well."

When you begin the communication process with positive comments, the feelings of goodwill they generate often remain throughout the entire conversation, and they help foster a more receptive environment whenever you must cover unpleasant, yet essential, topics.

POSITIVE COMMENT PREP

Because it's sometimes difficult to generate suitable and positive comments on the spur of the moment, it's helpful to have a few of these comments in mind beforehand. Think about each person with whom you will meet and ask yourself such questions as:

- What is this person's greatest strength?
- What things do I genuinely like about him or her?
- What interests does he or she have?
- What are his or her latest accomplishments?

Your answers don't have to be lengthy or profound, just brief and honest. For example, the person's greatest strength might be his promptness, you might genuinely admire her strong sense of fairness, or you might know that he is an avid athlete who recently participated in a local marathon. Once you have thought of a positive comment or two for each person, you will be prepared to begin your meeting on a positive note and have one less thing to worry about.

5. Practice Active Listening

Active listening is engaged listening. It requires paying close attention, making supportive comments, and asking pertinent

ACTIVE LISTENING
IS ENGAGED LISTENING

1. Meet in a place with few distractions.

2. Ask the other person to speak first and listen carefully to what they say.

3. Focus on the issues the person presents and try to view things from their point of view.

4. Make supportive and empathetic comments.

5. Ask clarifying, non-accusatory questions.

6. Restate what you believe was said.

7. Suggest solutions to any problems presented.

questions. Active listening requires several steps. First, arrange to meet when and where there will be few distractions. Once the meeting is underway and the introductory phase is complete, ask the person or people who requested the meeting to speak first, and listen carefully to what they say. Focus on the issues they present and try to see things from their point of view. As you listen, make supportive and empathetic comments (for example, "I can see why that would have upset you" or "You must have felt very relieved when you heard the news"), and ask questions to clarify your understanding of their concerns. Carefully word your questions so they are clear and non-accusatory in tone. (For example, "How much time does Jimmy spend each evening working on his mathematics homework?" versus "You said Jimmy hasn't been able to complete his mathematics homework because he doesn't understand the work. Can you tell me how much time he actually spends working on his mathematics homework each evening?") Once everyone has expressed their thoughts, restate in your own words what you believe was said. Then correct or clarify areas of misunderstanding, and if possible, suggest some solutions to any problems that were presented.

6. Emphasize Areas of Agreement

Since discussions are more enjoyable and make better progress when participants aren't at odds over every point, always try to emphasize areas of agreement. This is easy to do when an area of agreement is apparent, such as when you and a child's parents readily agree that the child needs additional help in math. Emphasizing an area of agreement can be most challenging, however, when all parties totally disagree.

Should you find yourself in such a difficult position, try to find the motivation behind the communicator's message and use that motivation as a basis for mutual agreement. For example, the parent of a tenth-grade student tells you he feels the material you are teaching his son isn't challenging enough. You can't agree with him because you are following the prescribed curriculum and test results confirm that the child is working to his ability level. The parent, however, persists in his demands that you teach his son more difficult subject matter. As you listen to the father, it becomes clear that he has a strong desire to see his son attend college and is concerned that the child won't be properly prepared to do so. Use the father's underlying motivation (his desire to have his son attend college) as the basis for mutual agreement, emphasizing that you too want to ensure that the young man is well prepared for college. Then explain how the current curriculum prepares students to meet that challenge and suggest that the parent and child meet with your school's guidance counselor to learn more about current college entrance requirements and academic standards. While the father still may insist that his child be given more challenging math work and you may have to work out some sort of compromise (see below), you have at least found an area of agreement to assure that the communication process moves forward.

7. Be Willing to Compromise

When the purpose of your communication is to resolve a problem, your willingness to compromise aids the dialogue and helps everyone arrive at a mutually acceptable solution. Compromise means conceding to alternative proposals.

For instance, a compromise with the father (from the previous example) who wants his son to have a more rigorous academic program might entail agreeing to any or all of the following courses of action:

- Provide the child with additional, academically challenging, non-credit homework assignments.

- Arrange a meeting with the father, a curriculum specialist, and you to review the prescribed curriculum and discuss how it prepares students for the academic demands of college.

- Request that the appropriate staff members (diagnosticians, psychometrists, counselors, reading specialists, school psychologists, and such) review the student's records to determine if further evaluation of his abilities and academic placement is warranted.

Compromise requires resourcefulness, maturity, and determination. It takes resourcefulness to think of viable problem-solving options, maturity to avoid counterproductive power struggles, and determination to work at a problem until it is resolved.

8. Respect Confidentiality

Because people are reluctant to discuss personal problems, express unpopular opinions, or disclose personal information if they feel their comments might be indiscriminately shared with others, your respect for confidentiality is essential to open and productive communication. You must not share with others the story little Tyler Tremont's mother told you about how Tyler's father was arrested for assault during a barroom brawl, or relate to them the hilarious reason April Adams' aunt gave you for April's three-week absence from school.

When you casually share privileged information it causes others to doubt your trustworthiness, and as a result, fear communicating with you. While people may find your anecdotes entertaining, they may quietly question your judgment and maturity for recounting them.

Disregarding confidentiality can cause legal problems as well. In fact, in cases involving confidential student records, teachers can be held legally liable for disclosing information about a child without the parents' permission. The exception to this is when child abuse is suspected. In such cases the law requires teachers to report their suspicions to the proper authorities without notifying the child's parents.

It is imperative, then, that you use good judgment when sharing with others any information that is shared with you. Be sure you know and follow your school system's policies and procedures regarding confidentiality, and make it a rule to keep personal information about your students and their families confidential, regardless of how insignificant that information may seem. When you are unsure if the information is personal, err on the side of caution and don't reveal it to others.

9. Avoid Gossip

The problem with gossip is that it can be such great fun and yet cause such great harm. Gossip will destroy trust and can tarnish your reputation as a responsible professional. Gossip is information of questionable accuracy, often spread by people who wish to do harm, and usually enjoyed by those who, for the most part, view gossiping as a form of innocent social entertainment. Once others judge you to be a gossip, however, they will hesitate to communicate with you openly and trustingly about any issue of value.

If someone confronts you with gossip and you do not wish to participate, yet feel compelled to reply, use one of the following responses.

A. Ignore the gossip and immediately change the subject to a positive, business-related topic.

> **Gossiper:** I just heard from someone in the know that Bob White's wife kicked him out of the nest last night!
>
> **You:** Good morning, Tina-Talker! You stopped by at just the right time. Take a look at Rupal Kellam's latest research report. Isn't this young man just brilliant? You know, I'm pretty sure he's going to get a full college scholarship!

B. React to the gossip with incredulity.

> **Gossiper:** Did you hear the latest scuttlebutt? Rumor has it that Mary Jones' mother slapped Principal Kellerman in the face during a parent conference yesterday afternoon.
>
> **You:** Oh, I can't believe that. It seems really farfetched to me. In the first place, Mrs. Jones doesn't seem like the aggressive out-of-control type, and in the second place, I can't imagine Mrs. Kellerman allowing a conference to go so badly that a parent would even think of physically attacking her.

BEWARE MORALE-BUSTING TOXIC GOSSIPS

No amount of tact will work with morale-busting toxic gossips. These are hardcore pessimists who live by the misery-loves-company philosophy of life. They are happiest when others around them are unhappy and take perverse pleasure in spreading rumors to make them so (cutbacks in staffing, transfers of beloved administrators, proposed salary cuts, and so forth.) Because they can quickly cast a pall over the most positive of days and use any comments you make (sometimes even those you don't make) to create more toxic gossip, it is best to steer clear of these cynical troublemakers.

C. Defend those being gossiped about.

Gossiper: Word is that Jim Jordan was just given an unsatisfactory teaching evaluation, and if his next evaluation isn't satisfactory, they're going to fire him.

You: That information can't be right. Jim's a good guy who's been working hard to improve his teaching and from what I've seen, his hard work has been paying off.

10. End on a Positive Note

If you end an exchange with hard feelings, it's difficult to establish positive and productive exchanges in the future. Work hard to end all communication on a positive note. You can accomplish this by making honest and tactful statements about the current situation, the need to continue communicating about the issue, your desire to resolve disagreements amicably, and your hope for good future outcomes.

For example, depending on the circumstances you might say:

- "I appreciate your effort to meet with me, Mr. and Mrs. Morgan, and I'm sure that by staying in touch and working together, we'll get Jamie back on the right track."

- "I'm sorry that we couldn't agree at this time on how to best help Millie control her angry outbursts, Mrs. Price. I know all of us want her to do well in school, and I hope you'll attend a meeting with the guidance counselor, the school psychologist, and me so we can devise an acceptable plan to help her."

- "It's unfortunate that Quincy hasn't earned a passing grade in algebra this marking period, but with extra tutoring help and all of us more closely monitoring his progress, his next quarter grade will most likely improve."

Part II
Tailoring Communication for a Perfect Fit

*S*uccessful teachers are effective communicators. They tailor their communication to fit the situation and use different styles and methods to fit their goals. These teachers understand that communicating with parents requires a somewhat different approach than communicating with administrators, and communicating with administrators typically requires a different approach than communicating with their teaching colleagues.

This section presents strategies to help you establish and maintain positive and clear communication with parents, administrators, colleagues, and community members, and explains how you can tailor the way you communicate to most effectively address specific situations.

Communicating With Parents

Successful K–12 teachers are skilled at communicating with parents: they understand that parental support and goodwill are essential to almost every child's school success, and they recognize that a big part of creating a positive and supportive parent–teacher relationship is through strong and effective communication. Effective communication with parents means initiating conversation with them early in the school year, informing them about significant classroom happenings, updating them regularly on their child's progress, and encouraging them to participate in school functions.

Initiating Communication With Parents

It is important to open clear lines of communication with parents early in the school year when everyone is optimistic and your initial contact can be positive and congenial. As the curriculum becomes more challenging and greater demands are placed on students, you will have already built strong relationships with parents that will enhance your chances of obtaining their understanding and support when the going might get tough. You can initiate contact with parents by phone, letter, email, or by inviting them to school for an introductory conference.

Initiating Communication by Phone

A telephone call gives you an opportunity to speak directly to parents without having to schedule face-to-face meetings at school. Phone them at the start of the school year, introduce yourself, speak with them about their child as an individual, and explain how they can get in touch with you if they have questions or concerns.

Before you make an introductory phone call, acquaint yourself with some general facts about the child. This material should be neither complex nor confidential, but rather information that you might use to support a brief conversation about their child as an individual. This might include things such as the child's birthday, special interests, number of siblings, and special awards.

When you call, identify yourself, inform them of the reason for your call, and inquire about the convenience of the call. If the call is inconvenient, apologize for the bother, ask them to suggest a better time for you to call, and quickly end the conversation. If the time is convenient, take care not to prattle on nervously but instead allow the parents to speak while you listen carefully to their comments. If the opportunity presents itself, use some of your previously gathered facts to comment about the child as an individual. Then, assure the parents that you wish to foster clear and positive communication with them throughout the school year, inform them of the best possible ways to contact you, and end by thanking them for their time and consideration.

OPENING THE DIALOGUE

If you're not sure what to cover during your initial conversation with parents, here are some topics you might want to consider:

- Your interest in the child—mention personal details such as the child's birthday, his or her special interests, or recent accomplishments.
- How excited you are to have their child in your class.
- The best ways for them to contact you.
- The best ways for you to contact them.
- When and how you will check in with them.
- Suggestions for how frequently they should check in with you and some reasons they might want to (i.e. "reports" of no homework for several days, graded test papers not finding their way home, etc.).

Quick Hint

Since parents and children often have different surnames, ask to speak with "the parents of" the specific child when phoning a parent for the first time. This will help you to locate the child's parent and avoid the possibility of inadvertently offending someone.

Initiating Communication by Letter

Because you may not be able to reach every parent by phone or your teaching load may make trying to do so impossible, it's always a good idea to send home a brief introductory letter. The great disadvantage of letters in lieu of phone calls, however, is that they don't provide an opportunity for you to interact directly with parents and react immediately to their questions, concerns, and comments. An introductory letter's great advantage, however, is that it provides written information that parents can refer to whenever they wish.

Initiating Communication by Email

When the parents of your students use email and have provided the school with their email addresses, it can be the most efficient way to send home an introductory letter or to make introductory comments. Take care when using email as a communication tool that parents who aren't computer-literate, or who don't have access to a computer, aren't made to feel left out or second-rate.

Initiating Communication by Meeting

Some schools set aside time in the school day for introductory conferences, during which teachers are expected to meet individually with parents, introduce themselves, inform the parents of the best ways to contact them, review classroom procedures and expectations, and answer any questions the parents might have regarding their child and the upcoming school year. Other schools have a general back-to-school gathering during which teachers are expected to meet with groups of parents, review goals and expectations for the coming year, and arrange for individual conferences at a later date.

SAMPLE OF AN INTRODUCTORY LETTER TO PARENTS

Dear Parent,

My name is Benjamin Lightfeather, and I want to introduce myself as your child's science teacher for this school year. I am really excited about teaching the newly revised hands-on science curriculum and am looking forward to working with you and your child. I want to prepare interesting science lessons that meet your child's educational and emotional needs, and I'd like to invite you to help by sharing any comments, suggestions, questions, or concerns you may have. You can reach me by calling the school (410-682-3242) and leaving a message or by emailing me at blfeath@acps.net. Be assured that I will return your call or email as quickly as possible, hopefully within the same day.

Thank you for your time, and I look forward to speaking with you in the future.

Sincerely,

Benjamin Lightfeather

Grade 8 Science Teacher, Parkside Middle School

Although these meetings take place early in the school year, it's important to prepare properly for them. First, ask several experienced staff members about the best way to dress, the usual format of the meeting, your exact role, and the type of material you are expected to cover.

For example, in many schools, the initial parent–teacher conference night is a rather formal event and teachers are expected to dress accordingly. Since the usual goal of these conferences is to give teachers an opportunity to meet with groups of parents and review goals and expectations for the coming year, you must be prepared to present goals and expectations that agree with those of your school district, and explain your school's policies and procedures should parents question them.

THE ADVANTAGE OF HOLDING A BACK-TO-SCHOOL NIGHT EARLY IN THE YEAR

Some schools schedule their annual Back-to-School night during the very first week of school. Although this early meeting places additional demands on teachers at a very busy time, it provides them with the perfect opportunity to open the lines of communication with parents, and saves them the time and effort they might otherwise expend on introductory phone calls and letters. Since these meetings are often brief and sometimes even a bit chaotic, it's important to stress the ways parents can contact you and that you welcome them doing so.

Keeping Parents Informed About Classroom Events

Since it's difficult for parents to be supportive of your efforts in the classroom when they know little about what's actually taking place there, make sure that you keep them informed about classroom happenings—especially positive classroom happenings. You can do this through your school's weekly or monthly parent bulletin, a student-created parent newsletter, and informative emails and notes.

The School-wide Parent Bulletin

If your school publishes a parent bulletin regularly, be sure it includes what's happening in your classroom. Depending on the guidelines and format, you might submit a variety of items:

- **Curriculum achievements:** Ms. Newmeister's third grade just completed their study of simple machines by working together in groups to create new machines using two or more simple machines. Their machines are on display in room 132.
- **Student accomplishments:** Missy Seymour won the monthly spelling bee by spelling the word "chaotic" correctly. The class voted Bobby Boyd "Citizen of the Week."
- **Special Activities:** The field trip to Reed Swamp Bird Sanctuary was a great success. In addition to learning from Ranger Roger about why such sanctuaries are needed, students spotted several different species of birds, including bald eagles, wild turkeys, and a great horned owl.

The Student-Created Newsletter

If your school doesn't issue a parent bulletin or if the bulletin's format doesn't allow for more than a general mention of classroom activities, you can have your students write their own newsletter. While it takes extra time and effort to produce a student-written newsletter and the project is usually better suited to elementary-level students, the effect it has on student pride, teaching opportunities, and parent interest make it a very worthwhile project.

Set aside some time during the later part of each month to review with your students the important class events that took place during that month. Help your students decide on the best information to include, and write the first issue as a class. Once the first issue is written, students can use it as a guide for writing succeeding issues, and depending on their age and ability level, different groups of students can be chosen (after the class decides on the important events to be included) to write the newsletter each month. The newsletter might contain curriculum achievements, student accomplishments, and special activities similar to those mentioned in the example of items to be included in the school-wide parent bulletin.

Informative Emails and Notes

If a monthly newsletter doesn't fit into your school's modus operandi or your students' maturity levels, keep parents informed of class happenings by sending home informative emails and hardcopy notes.

Updating Parents Regularly on Their Child's Progress

Not only do parents need to know what their child is doing in your class, they also need to know how well their child is doing. The formal way to let them know this information is through a report card. Reports cards are generally completed on a computerized form and issued quarterly. Because this format does not provide

Quick Hint

Unless you are certain that all parents have access to email, it's best to send information using both email and written notes. This helps assure that students who lack access to computers outside of school aren't singled out.

Before sending out multiple-recipient emails be sure that parents do not object to others having access to their email addresses.

timely details about the child's current progress or allow for interaction with the parent, it is not the best means of maintaining the most useful communication with them. Augment the quarterly report card by updating parents regularly on their child's progress. Do this by notifying parents when their child does exceptionally good work, having your students write notes home regarding their work in your class, informing parents of uncharacteristic changes in their child's performance, and devising a proactive plan for keeping parents of at-risk students well informed about their child's progress.

Notify Parents When Their Child Does Exceptionally Good Work

Notifying parents when their child does exceptionally good work is especially important for students who struggle or can be difficult. Doses of positive news go a long way toward forging solid, supportive relationships with parents, especially parents of challenging students. One way to do this is to have students choose two or three pieces from their week's work that they are proudest of, clip them together with an "I Am Proud of This" (or a similar title indicating the child's feeling of accomplishment) cover slip, and request that parents review the work and sign and return the cover slip. This will help build your students' confidence and highlight their greatest accomplishments for their busy but caring parents.

Have Your Students Write Notes Home Regarding Their Work in Your Class

Have your students write notes home regarding their work in class. Brainstorm with your students the kind of information they might include in their notes, and depending on the age and ability levels of your students, distribute a fill-in-the-blanks prototype to guide them through the process.

EXAMPLE OF A FILL-IN-THE-BLANKS PROTOTYPE NOTE

Dear Mom and Dad,

This note is to let you know what I'm learning in math class and how I think I'm doing.

We are learning about fractions. Three important things I have learned about fractions are: Fractions are parts of a whole thing. The bottom number of a fraction is called the denominator and the top number is called the numerator. When you add fractions, you only add the numerators.

The part I understand best is how to add fractions with the same denominators, but I'm having trouble adding fractions with different denominators. So far I've gotten a 95%, 75%, and 60% on my last three math quizzes.

Your daughter,

STUDENT NAME

Inform Parents of Changes in Their Child's Behavior or Academic Performance

Note changes in a child's behavior or academic performance and inform parents when those changes continue for more than a week. If the changes are significant, such as when an even-tempered child suddenly behaves in a hostile and belligerent manner or an honors student suddenly hands in totally unacceptable work, it's best to arrange to meet with the parents to discuss the problem. Otherwise, inform the parents by email or note and invite them to contact you if they wish to discuss the matter further.

EXAMPLE OF A NOTE OF CONCERN

Dear Mr. & Mrs. Johnson,

Over the past two weeks I've noticed a change in Jason's work habits in my World History class. He has failed to complete several classwork and homework assignments and hasn't been paying close attention during class discussions. While this may be just one of those temporary letdowns that all students experience during the course of a school year, if it were to prove otherwise and continue for an extended period of time, it could negatively affect Jason's understanding of world history and ultimately his World History class grade.

Please contact me if you would like to discuss Jason's progress in my class or if you might have some insight regarding the recent change in his efforts.

Sincerely,

Mr. Diluvian

Devise a Proactive Plan for Keeping Parents of At-Risk Students Well Informed

When a child has a documented history of learning and/or behavior problems, it's a good idea to meet with his or her parents early in the year and seek their input on how best to work with their child and how to keep them updated on their child's progress.

During your meeting you might ask parents questions such as:

• What were some of the things that teachers did in the past that worked with their child?

• What do they think is their child's greatest strength?

• What do they think is their child's weakness?

- What things make their child most comfortable?
- What are their major concerns as the school year begins?
- What is the best way to contact them?
- How frequently would they like feedback on their child's progress?
- What form would they like the feedback to take?

From the answers to these, you might learn that:

- The best way to avoid an ugly confrontation with an otherwise compliant reading disabled child is to call on her to read aloud only when she has had an opportunity to review and practice the passage beforehand.
- The child enjoys participating in class discussions.
- The parents would be most happy if you would email them a brief progress note every three to four days even if the note were to say their daughter is making satisfactory progress.

Communicating to Gain and Retain Parent Helpers

Between home and job responsibilities, today's parents are very busy people, and as a result, it's often difficult for teachers to find parents willing to chaperone field trips, assist in dressing the kids for the school play, or take on the gargantuan task of "classroom parent" for the school year. When teachers do find a responsible and conscientious parent volunteer, they frequently rely almost exclusively on that person until he or she says, "Enough, I'm not doing any more!"

While it's not always easy to get parents to volunteer to help out at school, especially in secondary schools, there are a few things you can do to gain and retain parents' help. Inform parents early in the school year of the kinds of help you will need, ask them personally for their help, support them when they provide help, and graciously acknowledge their assistance.

Make Parents Feel Welcome at School

The best way to ensure parents' involvement in school activities is to make sure they feel welcome at your school. Greet them when you see them in the halls even if they're not the parents of your students. When you know the parents, greet them by name, and if you can possibly do so, stop and chat for a minute or two. If a parent appears to be looking for a classroom, ask if you can direct them.

Depending on your school district's policies, whenever parents drop by during the school day, invite them into your classroom to see what's happening. When they do come in for a visit, introduce them to your students. Doing so protects parents from the stares of twenty-five pairs of curious eyes, models proper etiquette for your students, and makes everyone feel just a little more comfortable.

Inform Parents Early of the Help You Will Need

It's easier to get parents to agree to help with school activities if they are aware of them far in advance. During a PTA meeting early in the year, distribute a list of special activities you have planned for the year and invite parents to sign up to help out. When you make introductory phone calls or send out introductory emails, mention some of the special activities scheduled to take place during the year. Then mail or email them friendly reminders of those events as the year progresses.

Ask Parents Personally for Their Help

Parents are always more willing to help if you ask them personally. Talk with them individually after a PTA meeting, before a school performance, when they come to pick up their children after school, or through a personal email or note. Explain the project you are planning, how beneficial it will be for their children, and why extra help is needed.

Support Parents When They Provide Help

Once parents agree to help out, support them in their efforts. When they chaperone a group of students on a field trip, be sure to give them a trip itinerary and a copy of the student rules and expectations beforehand, and whenever possible, arrange for them to monitor groups of less challenging students. If you ask them to help tutor small groups of students, make certain they know exactly what to do and have all of the necessary materials to do it.

REPORT THE FACTS TO CURTAIL THE SPREAD OF HARMFUL RUMORS

When something goes wrong at school and your students witness a troubling incident such as an unpleasant altercation between adults or a serious fight between students, stop the spread of inaccurate Johnny-did-then-Janie-did-then-the-teacher-did recountings by informing parents of the facts as quickly as possible.

Unless your school has a policy that states someone else is to do so, contact parents as quickly as possible (preferably before the end of the school day) when their child has been involved in a major negative incident such as a fight or serious argument. Make it your policy to always return parents' phone calls and to promptly reply to their correspondence.

Graciously Acknowledge Parents' Assistance

When parents take the time and energy to assist you and your students, it's most important that their efforts be acknowledged. You can do this verbally or in writing, but it's best that you and your students do both. After telling parents how much their help is appreciated and giving them a round of applause, you can have your students write them thank you notes and write your own as they write theirs. Be sure to praise parent volunteers in your school or class newsletter, and if your school doesn't have one, organize a volunteer appreciation party. (This can be a relatively small affair organized by you and your students and held in your classroom, or a large affair organized by several teachers and their students held in a larger area of the school.)

Whether it's keeping them informed or asking for their help, an important part of every teacher's job involves communicating with parents. Teachers who cultivate good parent communication find that the support, understanding, and goodwill gained by their efforts make their jobs more doable and infinitely more pleasant.

Communicating With Administrators

It's essential that teachers communicate with their administrators. When and how often you do so depends on circumstances, your administrator's leadership style, and your own personality. Certain situations, such as those involving students' safety, require that you communicate immediately with administrators, while others, such as a request to switch committee assignments, do not.

Administrators with highly informal leadership styles happily interact with their teachers, have an open-door policy for meeting with them, and readily speak with anyone, anywhere. Administrators with strictly formal leadership styles, on the other hand, are less inclined to interact freely with their staff, require that teachers schedule meetings with them beforehand, and tend not to initiate casual conversations. The majority of administrators have leadership styles that fall somewhere between these two extremes.

The easiest way to determine an administrator's leadership style is to observe her carefully: people's actions reveal their leadership styles much more than anything they might say or write. For example, the administrator who says she is "always open to hearing teacher and staff comments and concerns," but consistently stays behind the desk in her office and meets with staff members only by appointment, actually functions under a much different leadership style than she purports. The administrator whose written directives lead recipients to conclude she has an authoritarian and rigid leadership style but whose personal interactions with her staff are always affable and accommodating has a similar effect: one that's hard to figure out.

Initiating Communication with Administrators

When you are new to a school, initiating communication with administrators isn't too difficult since they make every effort to meet and greet new teachers. Also, administrators usually meet with staff members individually several times throughout the year, and while the specific purpose for each of these meetings may differ (goal setting, review of progress, policies and procedures review, and so forth), the general purpose is to foster good communication and positive relationships with teachers.

Secondary schools usually require a different approach, however. Administrators in secondary schools typically cannot meet with individual staff members several times during the year. In large schools, the responsibility for maintaining effective communication with administrators is usually up to the teachers and staff.

If you are assigned to a large school with several administrators, open communication with each of them by introducing yourself at the very beginning of the school year. Once you learn which administrator is primarily responsible for your grade level or

QUESTIONS TO ASK YOUR ADMINISTRATOR

If your school issues a teacher's handbook, review it before meeting with your administrator and then ask questions to clarify and reinforce what you have read. If your school doesn't have a teacher's handbook or you don't have access to one before your first meeting, you might ask such questions as:

- How do I access curriculum guides?
- From whom should I seek mentoring help?
- What procedures should I follow to obtain equipment and supplies?
- What are the school's policies regarding student discipline?
- Is there a student handbook? How can I get a copy?
- How are teachers evaluated and who is involved in the evaluation process?
- What procedures must I follow if I must miss a day of school?

Remember that the beginning of the school year is very hectic for administrators; don't be upset if your administrator can't meet with you for several days. Even if you cannot quickly arrange a beginning-of-the-school-year meeting, your attempt to do so demonstrates your desire to communicate with your administrator.

A BETTER WAY TO SAY IT

What you say and how you say it during a meeting with your administrators depends on who initiates the meeting, the meeting's purpose, and the impression you wish to make. When administrators initiate a meeting, they will, in most cases, inform you of its purpose beforehand. They will then set the tone and will expect you to respond to their queries in a professional manner.

When you request a meeting with your administrators (or anyone else), your concerns are the primary focus. The way you choose to express yourself sets the meeting's tone and leaves your listeners with a lasting impression of you. For example, let's say two teachers, Ms. Green and Ms. Blue, each request meetings with their school's principal to discuss their constant loss of planning time due to schedule changes.

Ms. Green says, "I asked to meet with you, Mr. Preston, because I'm very upset. Every time we have a special event at this school, I lose my planning time. According to contract, all teachers are entitled to 250 minutes of planning time per week, but I never get my full 250 minutes, Mr. Preston, because you're always changing the schedule."

Ms. Blue says, "Thank you for taking the time to meet with me, Mr. Able. There's a problem I'm hoping you can help me resolve. For the past five weeks the schedule revisions for special events have reduced all first period classes by several hours, and I was wondering if there is some way revisions can be made so that first period isn't always cut from the schedule?"

Presenting concerns in an angry, confrontational manner, such as that used by Ms. Green, creates a negative tone, places the participants on the defensive, and causes hard feelings that can impede positive communication far into the future. Presenting concerns in a calm, non-confrontational manner, such as that used by Ms. Blue, creates a more hospitable tone, puts the participants at ease, and creates goodwill that often fosters future communication.

subject area, request a meeting to discuss your goals for the year and get "official" answers to any policies and procedures questions you may have. This is the perfect time to find out when and for what reasons you should contact the administration.

Maintaining Communication With Administrators

Maintain effective communication with your administrators by employing the golden rule and addressing their individual leadership styles. Greet them when you pass them in the halls, and whenever possible, pay them a sincere compliment or mention something positive that has happened in your school. This is not, as some would have you believe, "kissing up" to the boss. It is simply courteous and supportive behavior. Remember, no matter how self-assured your administrators may appear, they are still human and need positive feedback and encouragement just as you do. You are all on the same team.

It's also important to head off any potential problems before they become major administrative headaches by alerting your administrators to any disciplinary problems you've had to take action on that may cause repercussions at a higher level. If you confiscate Jordan Jones' MP3 player, for example, and you can't reach Mrs. Jones to explain why you did so, warn your administrators about the MP3 player incident before an angry Mrs. Jones contacts them. Also, since everyone makes mistakes, when you know you have erred, gather your courage and inform your administrators up front so they have a better chance to manage damage control. Although they may be upset with you at the time for making their job more difficult, your administrators will appreciate your honesty and respect your courage in the long run.

Evaluation Communications

No matter how busy your administrators or how little communication you've had with them, at some point during the year they will meet with you to evaluate your job performance. Depending on your administrator's leadership style, these meetings can be informal and collegial or formal and businesslike, but they almost always entail the sharing of pleasant as well as unpleasant news. For most teachers the pleasant news involves their professional strengths and the not-so-pleasant news involves their professional weaknesses.

Informal Versus Formal Evaluation Conferences

Informal evaluation conferences generally consist of a give-and-take, peer-to-peer discussion during which the administrator asks you to share your thoughts about your job performance, and at an opportune time during the discussion, uses your input to segue into his or her appraisal of your performance. Teachers are often more amenable to a discussion of their professional weaknesses during this type of conference since they usually (with the help of a few gently probing questions) broach the topic themselves.

Formal evaluation conferences often follow a set format during which the administrator offers his or her assessment of your professional strengths and weaknesses and allows you to make comments after the fact. The formal evaluation conference, as described here, is often more stressful to teachers because it affords them little chance to actually communicate with their administrator.

Be Prepared

Regardless of your administrator's leadership style and the type of evaluation conference he or she conducts, you can prepare for your conference by completing an honest self-assessment of your professional strengths and weaknesses beforehand. Most school districts provide teachers with self-evaluation checklists to help them with this process and many administrators require their teachers to write professional improvement goals and objectives they wish to meet during the school year. If you have access to these tools, make use of them. If not, ask yourself such basic questions as:

- Are my students learning the required curriculum?
- Do I prepare lessons that engage my students in the learning process?
- Do I treat all students with dignity and respect?
- Do I give my students useful feedback in a timely fashion?
- Is my classroom well organized for learning?
- Am I a good role model?
- Do I carry my fair share of non-teaching/support duties?
- Am I supportive of other staff members?
- Do I keep parents updated about their children's progress?

Dealing With Criticism From Your Administrator

Criticism from an administrator is an unavoidable and necessary part of your professional development, although it can be difficult to take. Administrators will, at times, critique your work and suggest steps you might take to improve it—it's their job to do so. Keep in mind that negative feedback can bring positive results only to those who are receptive enough to process the information, mature

STICK TO THE FACTS WHEN REPORTING PROBLEMS TO YOUR ADMINISTRATORS

When reporting problems to your administrators, state only observable facts and avoid emotionally charged language, value judgments, and unwarranted apologies. For example, a furious and out-of-control middle school student attempts to hit his teacher. The teacher grabs the student's arm to block the blow, and the student's jacket is torn.

The teacher reports the incident to the appropriate administrator immediately and as factually as possible. *"When Abe Eveson entered my classroom at the beginning of third period, he appeared to be very angry. He yelled, 'Yeah, dude, say it again, and you'll be visiting your friendly neighborhood orthodontist,' at a student in the hall. That student then replied with a comment that I couldn't hear, and Abe threw his knapsack on the floor and headed toward the door. I stepped in front of him to stop him from leaving the room and prevent what I believed would turn into a serious fight. He said, 'Get out of my way or I'll have to pop you, too!' and drew back his arm. As Abe's arm came forward, I grabbed it to keep from being hit, and as I did so, Abe's jacket tore."*

When recounting the incident to the administrator, the teacher avoids using emotionally charged language and judgmental statements such as hothead, dangerous, punk, thug, enraged, totally out of control, and so forth. The teacher also does not apologize for protecting himself nor does he make a statement that might be interpreted as wrongdoing on his part. He does not say, *"The whole fiasco was really my fault. I could see that Abe was angry and if I hadn't stepped in his way, none of this would have happened!"* Or, *"I think I may be responsible for tearing Abe's jacket, so if his parents want me to, I'll pay for a new one."*

enough to weigh it carefully, and perceptive enough to realize its value. Therefore, when your administrators critique your efforts, avoid becoming defensive and listen carefully to their comments (even if they are communicated in a painfully blunt style). Think about their directives and suggestions with an open mind, and recognize these directives as a condition of employment. Work to implement the suggestions that are well founded, as most will be. No matter how much your pride may be hurt, resist the temptation to vent to your colleagues about the unreasonableness and unfairness of an administrator's criticisms. Avoid placing them in an adversarial position, either to you or the administration, by polling them with don't-you-agree-with-me questions.

Communicating With Colleagues

You communicate with your colleagues on both personal and professional levels. Personal communication focuses on non-teaching issues, helps alleviate job-related stress, and can lead to long-term friendships. Professional communications, on the other hand, are formal exchanges that focus on important job-related information.

Making It Personal

Personal communication with your colleagues is very important: relationships you build with other teachers can be a strong source of support, information, and guidance throughout your teaching career. You can build effective personal relationships with your teaching colleagues by participating in informal faculty functions such as potluck luncheons, "poor Friday" breakfasts, after-school sports activities, talent shows, and so forth. Even if you are the shy and retiring type, supporting and attending a few of these fun faculty functions will help you earn the respect and affection of your fellow staff members, view your colleagues from a slightly different perspective, and open the lines of informal communication with them.

Foster communication with other teachers by learning everyone's name as quickly as possible; in a school with a very large staff, however, be sure to learn first the names of those colleagues with whom you work most often. Inquire about your colleagues' personal interests and tell them about yours. Listen attentively when they relate personal anecdotes and sympathetically when they share personal problems. Also, it's best to avoid heated discussions on emotionally charged topics such as politics and religion since they can result in misunderstandings and hard feelings that can hinder positive communication in the future.

Keeping It Professional

While effective personal communication is important to your well-being, effective professional communication is vital to your career success. If you fail to keep your fellow professionals informed about the needs of your students and the dynamics in your classroom, your students may miss out on essential support services such as extra help from instructional assistants, resource teachers, guidance counselors, and speech therapists, and you may miss out on mentoring and training sessions that can help you become a highly confident and competent professional. Also, failure to include your colleagues in job-related communication can create serious and long-lasting misunderstandings, not only with your colleagues, but also with parents and administrators.

Ask for Essential Job-Related Help When You Need It

Communicate with others to get essential job-related help. If you prepare viable lessons and do your best to teach them, but your students just aren't learning, communicate with the appropriate support people at your school. In some instances this communication must take place in writing before it takes place in person, such as when you must fill in a form requesting mentoring assistance. Explain as objectively as possible what's happening in your classroom, listen carefully to their comments and suggestions, and accept any classroom support they offer. For example, they might offer to do such things as: teach one group of students in your class while you teach the others; team teach some lessons with you; teach a model lesson to your class so you can observe good teaching techniques; or arrange for a particularly difficult student's case to be brought before your school's ARD (Admissions, Review, and Dismissal) team to determine if the child needs extra services with specialists. While you may be an independent and strong-willed person who eschews the assistance of others, or an anxious soul who's afraid of seeking assistance, keep in mind that your job is to provide the best possible education for your students—sometimes the only way to do your job well is to communicate your concerns and needs to others and accept their help.

AVOID THE SOCIALIZATION ADDICTION TRAP

Everyone needs a chance to socialize, and establishing personal relationships with your fellow teachers is important and healthy. But if you find yourself spending more time schmoozing with your fellow teachers than you do planning for or thinking about your teaching responsibilities, it's time to take a step back and re-evaluate your priorities. Re-evaluate if:

- You find yourself socializing in lieu of lesson preparation.
- Most of the conversations that take place during your socializing times are negative, highly critical of others, or contain off-color jokes or sexual innuendo.
- Your administrators do not have a high regard for the majority of those with whom you are socializing.

COMMUNICATING WITH THOSE WHO WORK BEHIND THE SCENES

School service workers (secretaries, custodians, cafeteria workers, school bus drivers, and such) keep a school running smoothly. Without these behind-the-scenes people, today's schools could not survive. Teachers who behave rudely to the secretaries or custodians will find themselves filling out payroll, attendance, and administrative forms in a cold, semi-dark classroom as they await thermostat repairs and light bulb replacements.

Make sure you communicate your respect for these unsung heroes and their work through both word and deed. It is respectful to thank the school secretary for correcting your attendance error before it becomes a problem for you. Furthermore it's also respectful (and much appreciated) to answer her phone when it's ringing off the hook and she's busy with another task.

Communicate respect for your school's service workers by:

- Addressing them by name.
- Speaking with them on a personal level (For example, inquiring about their families, personal interests, or health).
- Thanking them for the work they do.
- Complimenting them when they do a good job.
- Telling their supervisor when they do a good job.
- Listening carefully when they express a concern.
- Taking care not to create needless work or headaches for them. For example, have your students pick up after a "cut and paste" activity and make certain that your class is on time for lunch.
- Supporting them if they have a complaint about student behavior.
- Speaking directly to them if you have a complaint about their work and allowing them to correct the problem before you complain to the administration.

Communicate Essential Job-Related Information When You Know It

Maintain positive working relationships with others by including them in all job-related communications. When you schedule a meeting with a child's parents, be sure to inform your colleagues who also teach the child about the meeting and invite them to attend. (Also, be sure to let the parents know beforehand that some of their child's other teachers might attend the meeting.)

If you know of a change in your schedule that will impact other teachers' schedules (for example, a crucial lesson or a rehearsal for a school performance that is running long and will cause your students to be late for their next class), let the other teachers know as soon as possible. When you chair a committee, regardless of how informal the group dynamics are, be certain everyone involved is given a schedule of meeting dates and times and a copy of each meeting's minutes.

To avoid serious misunderstandings, don't make job-related commitments for others. For example, if you meet with a child's parents and promise them the school guidance counselor (who is unaware of the meeting) will provide services to their child, the counselor may be more than a little peeved with you. This places him in the unenviable position of explaining to the child's parents and the administrators (to whom the parents complained) that he cannot add another student to his already overbooked schedule. If you tell a child's parents that paying for a reading tutor is unnecessary because the school employs a reading specialist, this may place the reading specialist in an uncomfortable position because she was not given the opportunity to explain why she couldn't help this particular child. This leaves the reading specialist with a sense that your comments may have cast her professionalism in a bad light.

To avoid professional communication breakdowns:

- Invite all colleagues who may have relevant information to share to conferences.

- Avoid making commitments for others.

- Instruct those who want additional services for a child such as speech therapy, counseling, reading tutoring, and so forth to make arrangements directly with the service provider.

- Inform staff members when matters of concern to them are discussed during a conference they did not attend. For example: Tell the school custodian that a parent praised the cleanliness of the school building, and make the football coach aware that a parent voiced concern about the "crude and crass" language used by the football team during practices.

Communicating With the Community

A school is viewed either favorably or unfavorably by the community it serves based on the accomplishments and behavior of its students and staff, both inside and outside of the school setting. Schools develop reputations not just because of what takes place within their buildings, but also because of the overall effect they have on their surrounding communities.

Schools with good reputations have students and staff members who show consideration for their communities through direct and indirect communication. They speak respectfully to residents, treat their property with care, and are sensitive to their community's needs and concerns. Schools with good reputations attract and keep better students.

Your school's success is linked to its status within the community. That's why positive and open communication between your school and your community is so important; your school will be judged based on the public interactions you and your students have with its community. As a teacher, there are several steps you can take to foster positive communications between your school and the community.

Closely Monitor Your Students' Behavior During Field Trips and School Outings

Large groups of unsupervised students can easily wreak havoc on museums, souvenir shops, restaurants, and other public facilities, leaving behind stressed-out employees, damaged merchandise, and unfavorable impressions. Set firm guidelines for these excursions, and respond immediately when a student displays unacceptable

FOILING FIELD TRIP FIASCOS

A successful and trouble-free field trip requires good planning and excellent communication. First, find out exactly what your students will see and do on the trip by reviewing information packets about your destination; talking with other teachers who have taken similar field trips; and when possible, taking a preliminary trip yourself. Use some class time to convey this information to your students. For example, if you know that they will take a guided tour of your local historical society, prepare them for the experience by explaining how the tour will be conducted and giving them a brief overview of what they will see. Finally, and most importantly, review with your students your behavioral expectations for the trip and the consequences for not meeting those expectations.

Because proper student conduct during school outings is essential to good community relations and student safety, many schools have a list of school-wide behavioral guidelines for field trips that all students and teachers must follow. Other schools have students and their parents sign a field trip contract stating what is acceptable and expected behavior during the trip and agreeing to follow the rules.

behavior. Take the necessary steps to exclude any student whose behavior on past trips was unacceptable or have a parent accompany and take responsibility for the child on future trips.

Be Cooperative With the People Who Live Near Your School

Acknowledge neighborhood residents with a friendly greeting if you see them while traveling to and from school. If faculty parking is limited and you must park on neighboring streets, take care not to block driveways or otherwise inconvenience residents, and remind parents to be considerate of neighbors when picking up and dropping off their children at school. It's also helpful to ask your students to remind their parents to be good neighbors.

Stress to Your Students the Importance of Respecting the Properties Neighboring Their School

Talk with your students about the importance of respecting surrounding properties. Demonstrate through role playing the feelings of frustration and anger that others can have when their property is mistreated, and explain how even a few people with these feelings can create a poor reputation for your school. Formulate with your students some guidelines they can follow to show respect for the property neighboring their school.

Use Good Judgment When You Communicate With the Public About School-Related Issues

While you can help build good public relations between your school and its community through satisfactory communications, you can also create serious public relations difficulties by indiscriminately sharing privileged in-school or confidential student information with those outside of your school. Avoid such difficulties by following these four basic rules whenever you communicate with the general public: share in-house information judiciously, make definitive statements with care, resist invitations to criticize your

EXAMPLE OF STUDENT RESPECT FOR NEIGHBORING PROPERTY GUIDELINES

Your behavior both inside and outside of Woodrow Wilson High School reflects on your school and shapes its reputation. If you want to attend a school with an excellent reputation, you must create that reputation by not only doing well in school, but by showing consideration and respect for the community around the school. The easiest way to do this is to follow a few common-sense rules when traveling to and from school.

- Do not throw trash on neighboring properties.

- Avoid using slang and expletives.

- Do not run through flower gardens, damage shrubs and bushes,
  or sit on cars.

- Keep the volume on radios, boom boxes, compact disk players, and such to a level that only you and your friends can hear.

- If you drive to school, obey the speed limits and do not block driveways or disregard parking restrictions.

colleagues, and disclose information about your students only to authorized people.

Share In-house Information Judiciously

When conflicts become public between faculty members and a school's administration regarding policies on student discipline, curriculum, non-teaching duties, and class size, it's not unusual for parents and the news media to ask teachers about the controversies. If you are faced with these kinds of questions, reply with diplomacy and discretion, regardless of how earnest the questioner, or how seemingly inconsequential the question. You might say, for example, "I'm sorry but I really don't have enough information on this matter to make an informed comment." Also, it's wise to decline comment on politically charged issues such as school redistricting, the implementation of No Child Left Behind policies, or the appropriateness of a newly proposed sex education curriculum. Instead, direct questioners to speak with your school's administrators since they have the most up-to-date and accurate information on these matters.

Make Definitive Statements with Care

Be sure you are correct when making definitive statements, and if possible, avoid such statements altogether. There is a world of difference between "None of my students got near the neighbors' cars during recess," and "As far as I could tell, none of my students got near the neighbors' cars during recess." While the former is definitive and can cause confusion and anger if it proves to be inaccurate, the latter qualifies your comment and helps avoid future misunderstandings.

Resist Invitations to Criticize Your Colleagues to Community Members

Resist the temptation to criticize or comment on your teaching colleagues to others in the community, regardless of how much you may be encouraged to do so. Even what may seem to you to be completely innocuous comments can be misinterpreted or passed along incorrectly by others. Remember that whether you are in the classroom or at a community function, you are a de facto spokesperson for your school and the people in it, so be careful about getting involved in conversations with community members that could potentially be misinterpreted or construed as negative.

Disclose Information About Your Students Only to Authorized People

It is of paramount importance that you share information about a child with only the appropriate professionals and the child's parents or legal guardians. While this might seem obvious, there are instances when you can easily be lulled into commenting improperly.

For example, you bump into a parent while shopping at the grocery store, and during the course of your conversation, the parent comments, "I understand Stuey Smith, the new kid in your class, started that terrible fight in the cafeteria at school yesterday." And you reply, "Well, Stuey does have a volatile temper, but I'm not sure if he was involved in the fight."

You have unthinkingly shared confidential information about a child (Stuey has a volatile temper) with an unauthorized person. Even though the most casual of observers might readily conclude that Stuey has a serious problem controlling his temper, that information is listed in Stuey's confidential records, and as his teacher, you must keep this information classified.

If you are faced with questions regarding student confidentiality, tactfully refuse to answer and redirect the conversation to an appropriate topic. Faced with the Stuey Smith comment from the previous example, you might say, "Yes, that really was some fight, but I believe Principal Harkins has found the guilty parties and is dealing with them. Speaking of the cafeteria, have you heard about the healthier menu the school is offering to students?"

Publicize Your Students' Successes

Whenever your students do something that's noteworthy, be sure the word gets out into the community. Publicize their positive accomplishments in the school newsletter, and (with your administrator's blessing) notify the community newspapers or your school system's public relations officer of these happenings. Encourage your students to enter such community-sponsored education competitions as essay contests, science fairs, and art shows, and prompt them to participate in charitable fundraising events.

Ask the Community for Its Help

With your administrator's permission, ask community service groups (such as Kiwanis Clubs, Chambers of Commerce, and Optimist Clubs) for their assistance with school projects such as science fairs, flea markets, auctions, and car washes, and solicit responsible community members to mentor students. Activities such as these can give students and the members of a community group an opportunity to interact and get to know each other on a more personal level.

Part III

Communicating With Difficult People

*R*egardless of how well you hone your communication skills, there will be times when difficult people will challenge them. Although communication with angry parents, dictatorial administrators, passive colleagues, and obstinate school service workers follows the same general guidelines covered earlier in this book, they often require additional insight and specialized modifications to be most effective.

In this section we'll address apecific situations and analyze the strategies at work. Particular points to keep in mind with each type of situation will allow you to communicate effectively even with the most challenging people.

Communicating Effectively With Angry People

Since it is nearly impossible to communicate effectively when people are extremely angry, it's best to prevent them from becoming so. You can do this by following the steps to building effective communication explained in Part I. However, if you are confronted by someone who is angry, try the following strategies to establish productive communication with them.

STRATEGIES FOR COMMUNICATING EFFECTIVELY WITH ANGRY PEOPLE

Anger is a fact of life. Everyone gets angry at one time or another. The trick to dealing with angry people is to refuse to become angry yourself. When communicating with angry people you should:

- Remain calm and stay as objective as possible.
- Move to a more private venue if you are confronted in a public place.
- Allow the person to vent within the standards of acceptable conduct.
- Validate the person's concern by restating it in your own words.
- Offer a sincere apology when it is called for.
- Ask the person how he or she would like to see the problem resolved.
- Find a point of common agreement.
- Arrive at a mutually acceptable solution.
- End the discussion cordially.

Remain Calm and Stay Objective

This is easy to recommend but difficult to do, especially if the angry person is very upset. It's helpful to focus on the fact that we all get angry at times and sometimes we even rant excessively. In the vast majority of cases, however, we all get over our anger. While encountering someone who is angry may be momentarily unpleasant, if you manage the experience carefully it can result in such positive outcomes as clearer communication, more realistic expectations in the future, and some sort of peaceful agreement.

Move to a More Private Venue

When an angry person with a legitimate concern confronts you in a public place, calmly, but not arrogantly, suggest that your conversation take place in a more private venue. You might say, for example, "I can see you are very upset that Suzy Q wasn't selected for the Quill and Scroll Society, Mrs. Q. Why don't we go to my classroom where I can explain the selection process and address your concerns without interruption?"

Sadly, people who enjoy flexing their irritability muscles in public are usually reluctant to move to a more private area and will simply ignore or refuse your suggestion. If you are faced with such a person, calmly and firmly inform her that you are most willing to speak with her regarding her concern, but will only do so in a place that is less public. Then turn and walk to that area. The angry person will likely follow you. If she doesn't follow you, do not turn around; go immediately to an administrator and inform him about what is going on.

Allow the Person to Vent

Once you are in a more private area, allow the person to vent. Venting doesn't mean you should tolerate verbal abuse or foul language. The most effective way to stem an angry torrent is to calmly and respectfully call the person on it. For example, you could say, "I realize you are very upset, Mrs. McPherson, but I'm not yelling or swearing at you and I'd like for you to do the same for me."

If the angry person continues to vent in an abusive and offensive manner, terminate the meeting. Inform the angry person that you feel she is too upset to discuss the issue and that you will be happy to meet at a later time when she is less upset. Then politely excuse yourself and leave the area.

Validate the Person's Concern by Restating It

The surest way to calm an angry person is to communicate to her that you understand the reason for her ire. Listen carefully without interruption as she presents her side of the story. Then, repeat her concern back to her in your own words. For example, you could say, "You're upset because I've missed several committee meetings." Restating a person's complaint in your own words is not necessarily an admission that you agree with it, but doing so helps mollify the other person and clarifies the problem in your own mind.

HOW TO RESTATE AND VALIDATE

If you listen carefully to their comments, it's fairly easy to restate and validate others' concerns even when they confront you unexpectedly. As the person speaks, try hard to disregard and ignore any unjust and unwarranted criticisms of you, and control the urge to become defensive. Focus instead on the person's description of the injury she feels she has experienced. Listen for key, emotionally charged words that describe the hurt (such as embarrassed, insulted, bullied, physically injured, and so forth). When the person finishes voicing her complaint, restate her concern using the key "hurt" words she used in her description and validate her feelings by making comments such as, "I'm sure it was upsetting when little Janie came home crying," or "You must have felt really scared when Sean walked in the door with blood on his shirt and, once you knew he was okay, very angry that someone hit him in the nose."

Offer a Sincere Apology When It is Called For

If you realize that you have made a mistake after hearing the angry person's side of the story, offer a sincere apology. If the person is very upset, and you can't agree that you have made a mistake, it is helpful to offer the generic, "I'm sorry you are so upset about this," or, "I'm sorry we can't agree on this matter."

Ask the Disgruntled Person
How Best to Resolve the Problem

After the angry person has calmed down and is more receptive to discussing the problem, ask her how she would like to see the problem resolved or for suggestions as to how it might

THE CULPABILITY CONUNDRUM

In large school systems new teachers are often warned by administrators, school district lawyers, insurance underwriters, and teachers' organizations not to make careless comments that might be misinterpreted as admissions of wrongdoing. These could, unfortunately, result in lawsuits against the teachers, their administrators, and their school district. While this advice may seem insensitive and cynical, it addresses a sad reality of today's litigious work world, and therefore should be carefully considered.

For example, if a student falls and breaks her leg playing soccer during recess and you feel compelled to offer her distraught parents a sympathetic apology, you would not do so in a way that might be interpreted as an admission of wrong-doing on your part, but rather you would offer an apology that is a simple statement of fact. Instead of the conscientiously emotional and legally vulnerable statement, "I feel so badly that Inez fell and broke her leg, Mrs. Hernandez. I wish I had stopped the game before this happened," you would offer an apology simply stating observable facts: "I'm so sorry that Inez fell and broke her leg, Mrs. Hernandez."

be prevented in the future. Realize that an angry and upset person often doesn't want or expect any resolution other than an empathetic listener. However, if she does suggest a viable solution, accept it graciously. If her solution is unacceptable, tactfully explain why it is so and work with her to arrive at a more workable solution.

For example, a parent who is angry because his son has missed the afternoon school bus several times might suggest that the best way to keep his child from missing the bus is to dismiss him first every day. The teacher explains that this solution is not practical because he rewards students who are prepared to leave promptly at the end of the school day by dismissing them first. He calmly and assertively tells the father that he cannot reward his son for not following the class guidelines. He then suggests as an alternate solution: he will "buddy up" the bus-missing child with a student who is always prepared for dismissal and have that student help the slower child be prepared for dismissal.

Find Points of Common Agreement

During the course of your discussion, look for points of common agreement you can use to come up with a mutually acceptable solution. If the displeased person suggests a solution that is unacceptable to you, use some part of it (even if just a tiny kernel) to create an alternative solution. On the other hand, if you suggest a solution that is completely unacceptable to the other party, revise it so that it addresses his or her concerns in some way. For instance, in the previous example, the father's suggested solution was unacceptable to the teacher, but he agreed with the father's basic premise: If the child was going to catch the bus on time, he had to get out of the classroom more quickly.

Work to Fashion a Mutually Acceptable Solution

Once you establish a point of common agreement, regardless how simple or obvious it is, use it as a basis to work out a mutually acceptable solution. In the case of the late child, the teacher doesn't find the father's solution workable, yet he finds an obvious point of agreement in its basic premise and uses that to come up with a mutually acceptable solution.

End the Communication Cordially

This is an easy step to accomplish in the case of a meeting that ends well. But even if the conversation was unpleasant and you were unable to arrive at a mutually acceptable solution, it is still possible to end it cordially. Simply state that you are sorry that you and the other party are unable to agree and suggest that all involved meet with a third party (for example, a department chair, administrator, or supervisor) who might offer some fresh perspectives and help resolve the issue.

The Strategies at Work: The Peeved Parent

It's late on a Monday afternoon and Mrs. James, a third-grade teacher at Benjamin Franklin Elementary School, is preparing to leave for the day when an obviously angry parent arrives at her classroom door.

"Mrs. James, I want to know why you hurt my daughter Kerry's feelings so badly that she came home sobbing and said she was never going back to your classroom again!" the parent demands.

Mrs. James is totally surprised by the parent's sudden visit and angry demeanor. She pauses to collect herself and then replies calmly, "I know you're very upset because something hurt Kerry's feelings, Mrs. Johnson. Come on in and tell me what happened."

"That's just it, Mrs. James, I don't really know what happened. It's your classroom. You should be able to tell me what happened. All I know is that Kerry came home upset and crying. She told me that just before dismissal, you made fun of her in front of the whole class and she never wanted to go back to your class again."

"Oh, Mrs. Johnson," explains Mrs. James evenly, "I think I know the incident that upset Kerry, but I had no idea she was upset and

embarrassed! It was the end of the day and everyone was packing up their things to go home. The noise level in the room was rising and I didn't want students to miss the announcement for their busses so I directed everyone to stop talking and take their seats. Everyone followed my directions, but Kerry was so engrossed in a conversation she was having with two of her friends that she didn't hear what I said and continued talking long after the room had grown absolutely silent.

When she realized that she was talking to the silent class she looked so startled that everyone in the class laughed, myself included. I'm afraid that may be what embarrassed Kerry so badly."

"Yes, I'm sure having everyone in the class, including the teacher, make fun of her was the height of embarrassment for Kerry!" fumes Mrs. Johnson.

"No one made fun of Kerry. No one mocked her or ridiculed her," explains Mrs. James gently but emphatically. "It was just a funny incident that I believed was over as quickly as it happened. Obviously, I totally misinterpreted its importance to Kerry. For that I am truly sorry. What do you think I might do to set things straight with her?"

"Well, I can't really say, Mrs. James, because Kerry is very sensitive and her feelings are really hurt," replies Mrs. Johnson thoughtfully.

"Suppose I meet with her first thing tomorrow to tell her that I'm sorry about this misunderstanding and try to help her see that she has no reason to feel so embarrassed?" offers Mrs. James.

"Well, I guess it wouldn't hurt for you to try. You know Kerry is small for her age and very sensitive. I won't stand by and see her hurt."

"Yes, Mrs. Johnson, I know Kerry is a very sensitive child, but she's also very bright, and has much to offer, and I'm sure we both want to resolve this problem as soon as possible. So, I'll be sure to speak with Kerry first thing tomorrow morning and explain to her that the class and I were laughing at a funny situation and not making fun of her. Also, I'll give you a call tomorrow evening to let you know how my talk with Kerry turned out."

"Well, okay then," replies the mollified Mrs. Johnson. "I just hope this doesn't happen again."

"Neither do I," responds Mrs. James, silently resolving that throughout the school year she will help Kerry Johnson be less sensitive and her mother less protective.

Analyzing the Communication Process

Special Considerations

Communicating with angry parents can be one of the most difficult tasks a teacher faces. This is because teachers get caught between the wants of children and the wants of parents. Children instinctively want to gain their parents' attention and approval, and parents instinctively want to ensure their children's well being. It's not surprising, then, that children try to gain their parents' attention by recounting classroom events in an exaggerated and skewed fashion. Depending on the incident and the degree of embellishment, a recounting can result in the parents angrily demanding an explanation from the befuddled teacher, who then must attempt to assuage their anger by tactfully presenting a more balanced picture of the events in question.

Examining the Strategies

Mrs. James first listens objectively to the angry parent's complaint, and then focuses on the reason the parent feels her child's well-being was jeopardized. Mrs. James then validates the parent's concern with the empathetic and relevant comment, "I know you're very upset because something hurt Kerry's feelings." This is a non-judgmental and non-committal comment that restates the parent's reason for concern (her daughter's feelings were hurt). It also relates to the mother's desire to protect her child (the mother is angry because her daughter was hurt). The initial comment restating the problem and validating the parents' protective instinct calms her anger and opens the lines of communication.

Once the parent is calm and appears receptive, Mrs. James offers her explanation of the events in question. She gives an accurate and objective account of the incident from her perspective, refraining from the use of emotionally charged words that can easily renew the parent's feelings of anger (words such as raucous, bizarre, helpless, bully, crazy, shy, aggressive, and so forth.) She carefully describes the mitigating circumstances that took place during the incident, such as classroom dynamics at the day's end. Mrs. James' description of circumstances is free of complaints, excuses, and statements that might be interpreted as a lack of professional competence. She does not say that she is prone to migraines and was fighting the onset of one at the time of this episode, nor did she say the class comprises the most challenging group of students the school has ever encountered. She instead explains the situation in her classroom at the time of the problem in a forthright and unemotional fashion.

After Mrs. James completes her explanation, she offers an appropriate and honest apology for the misunderstanding. She then asks the parent to suggest solutions to the problem, proposes some viable solutions to address the problem, and agrees to meet with the embarrassed student to clear the air.

Hints and Reminders

When communicating with peeved parents:

- Stay calm and allow the parents to vent.

- Listen carefully to their concerns.

- Give an accurate and objective account of the event/problem from your perspective.

- Unemotionally recount any mitigating circumstances and avoid offering them as whiny excuses. (For example, "The buses were an hour late coming back from the field trip because of a road construction traffic tie-up" as opposed to "Well, it certainly wasn't my fault that we sat in a fifteen-mile traffic back-up for over an hour!")

- Offer a sincere apology if one is called for.
- Ask how the parents would like to see the problem resolved.
- Propose a viable solution or arrange for the parents to speak with someone who can further address their concerns.

Worries and Warnings

Sometimes parents may remain unreasonably confrontational and angry despite your best efforts to placate them. If this happens, calmly suggest that since they are still very upset about a particular incident, they should address their concerns to your administrator. For example, you might say, "Mr. and Mrs. Peevy, I can see that you are still quite angry about this whole unfortunate incident. Perhaps you would like to speak with Mrs. Meadows, the school principal."

There may also be times when you just can't think of viable solutions for a problem. When this happens tell the parent that you need some time to come up with some possible solutions and set up an appointment.

The Strategies at Work:
The Annoyed Administrator

It's lunchtime at Martin Luther King Elementary School and Mr. Pradhan, a fourth-grade teacher, has just dropped off his class at the cafeteria and is heading into the faculty room when Ms. Hepburn, the school principal, stops him.

"I need to speak with you for just a minute, Dan. Could you come to my office please?" says Ms. Hepburn.

"Sure," replies Mr. Pradhan, puzzled by Ms. Hepburn's request.

Once in her office, Ms. Hepburn says, "Dan, I'm concerned that every day for the past two weeks your class has been late for lunch and this cannot continue. I want you to realize," Ms. Hepburn continues, her face coloring and voice rising, "that when your class is late, it backs up every class behind yours in the serving lines and creates unnecessary disciplinary problems!"

Mr. Pradhan pauses for a minute to collect his thoughts and then says, "I'm sorry our being late has caused others such problems. I didn't realize that we were having such a negative impact on everyone else. We've been combining our Language Arts and Social Studies units right before lunch and my kids are researching, writing, and producing a play about the Underground Railroad. It's hard to get them to stop and clean up on time, but I understand the problem, and I promise you they won't be late for lunch again!"

"Well, I'm sure you'll keep your promise, Dan. And I hope you'll invite me to the premiere of that play," states the appeased principal.

"We sure will. The publicity team was working on invitations right before lunch today!" replies the relieved Mr. Pradhan.

Analyzing the Communication Process

Special Considerations

Administrators evaluate their staff members in most school districts. Teachers who enjoy and want to retain their positions must seriously consider their administrators' comments, concerns, and criticisms. If administrators express annoyance with you, consider the many job-related demands and pressures they face, and don't take their comments as personal insults or attacks. View them instead as opportunities to learn and grow professionally, or opportunities to correct mistakes that otherwise might eventually hurt your success as a teacher.

Examining the Strategies

The teacher, Mr. Pradhan, is polite and agreeable when Ms. Hepburn asks to speak with him. He quells his impulse to say, "This is my duty-free lunch time and you'll have to meet with me later," because he knows from experience that Ms. Hepburn only invites teachers to her office when she has something important to say. He listens attentively as Ms. Hepburn presents her concern, validates it through restatement, and offers an honest and sincere apology for his mistake in judgment. He does not ask his principal to suggest solutions for the problem since the solution is implied in her comment, "This [the lateness to lunch] cannot continue!" He then explains the positive teaching circumstances that caused his class to be late and assures Ms. Hepburn that the problem is solved.

Hints and Reminders

When communicating with annoyed administrators:

- Remain calm and try to view the situation realistically. (Your administrator may just be having a really bad day and your transgression may have been the last straw.)
- Be polite and professional.
- Avoid emotionally charged language and overstatements such as ridiculous, insulting, stupid, impossible, intolerable, and so forth when explaining your actions.
- Offer a sincere apology when one is called for.
- If you have erred, vow that you will do your best not to make the same mistake again.

Worries and Warnings

Annoyed administrators tend to become even more upset when staff members (and students) try to blame their mistakes on others. If you offer an explanation for your actions, own up to and apologize for any mistakes you made.

The Strategies at Work: The Cranky Colleague

It's early on a Tuesday morning and Amy Wexler, a second-year teacher at West Side Middle School, is busy at her desk in the small planning room that she shares with two other "floaters," teachers who are not assigned permanent classrooms and must "float" into whatever rooms are free throughout the day. Marian Fox, a longtime West Side faculty member, arrives at her door.

"Amy, I need to speak with you about a concern I have," Ms. Fox says somewhat curtly.

"Okay," Ms. Wexler replies apprehensively.

"Amy, you absolutely must do something about the disgraceful way your fourth-period class leaves my classroom. When I leave my room at the end of the third period, everything is in good order; the desks are straight and the floor is clean. But when I return for fifth period, the place looks like a disaster area!

I really wasn't going to say anything to you about this. But yesterday, one of your students, the kid who sits in the third row, put a huge wad of bubble gum under the desk and it got all over Timmy Tyler's clothes. You know, Timmy Tyler, the kid whose dad is on the school board! Well, that was the last straw! You're just going to have to make sure that your kids leave my classroom in better order because if this continues, I'm going to have to complain to the office!"

Ms. Wexler is surprised and somewhat shaken by the older teacher's forceful manner. She takes a deep breath to calm herself and collect her thoughts before replying, "I'm sorry that you think my students always leave your classroom a mess, but I'm afraid I can't agree with you."

"Can't agree with me?!" interrupts Ms. Fox.

"Please, Marian, let me finish. I didn't interrupt you, and I'd appreciate it if you'd give me the same courtesy."

"Okay, but your kids do always leave my room a mess!" persists Ms. Fox.

Ms. Wexler disregards Ms. Fox's comments and replies, "Marian, because I'm a floater, I have to be ready to move quickly to my next *class. I always end my classes five minutes early and have my students clean up their areas and straighten their desks. And, for the most part, they comply.*

"As far as the gum under the desk," Ms. Wexler continues, taking out a seating chart and attendance record, "I think the student assigned to that seat was absent yesterday."

"Well, that doesn't mean some other student of yours didn't put the gum there!" counters Ms. Fox.

"That's true," replies Ms. Wexler, "but it doesn't necessarily have to be one of my students. I'm not trying to be difficult, Marian. It's just that I take great pains to respect the classrooms I float into, and I try to teach my students to do the same. I can't help but disagree with your assessment of the condition your room is left in every day. If you feel it's necessary to discuss your concern with the administration, I'll be glad to go with you."

"Well, I can't do it today, but perhaps sometime later this week," suggests Ms. Fox. "In the meantime, I hope you'll work a little harder at keeping my classroom in order."

Analyzing the Communication Process

Special Considerations

Communicating with angry teaching colleagues differs from communicating with angry parents and administrators, because colleagues do not necessarily require the same degree of deference and sensitivity. When a fellow teacher expresses displeasure, you have the choice of taking their complaint seriously or discounting it. Regardless of your decision, it's still best to employ at least some of the steps to communicating effectively with angry people outlined previously in order to keep peaceful relations with your fellow colleagues. To do otherwise is to create negative working relationships that might extend long into the future.

Examining the Strategies

The young teacher, Ms. Wexler, listens attentively as the more experienced teacher, Ms. Fox, states her complaint. She does not interrupt to make conciliatory or defensive remarks. When Ms. Fox finishes, Ms. Wexler pauses to think before speaking and then calmly explains why she feels she cannot address her colleague's complaint. When Ms. Fox interrupts her explanation, Ms. Wexler assertively yet politely insists on courteous treatment. She ends her part of the discussion by agreeing to go with Ms. Fox to discuss the problem with the administration. By doing so, she is informing Ms. Fox that she feels her complaint is unwarranted and she does not fear speaking with the administration about it.

Hints and Reminders

When communicating with a cranky colleague:

- Stay even-tempered and upbeat.
- Refuse to be drawn into an argument.
- Listen carefully to what your colleague has to say.
- Explain your side of the story.
- Offer an apology if one is warranted.
- If you disagree with your colleague's analysis of the problem, say so.
- Agree only to solutions that you find equitable.

Worries and Warnings

While there are times when it may be absolutely essential for you to deal with your teaching colleagues in a highly assertive manner, those times should be few and far between. Teachers who assert to others what they will and will not do often find they have undermined their personal support systems.

If you are very upset about something a colleague has or hasn't done, step back and give yourself time to view the situation more objectively before making strongly assertive statements. It's also wise to remember that in a hierarchical system such as education, today's teaching colleague may well be tomorrow's administrator.

The Strategies at Work: The Crabby Custodian

It's five o'clock on a Monday afternoon and Vicky Chow is working in her classroom at John Kennedy High School when Ed Parker, the custodian assigned to clean her area, enters the room pulling a cleaning cart and vacuum cleaner.

"Man, this place looks like a bomb went off in it," Ed complains as he dumps the overflowing trashcan into a larger trash bin and drops the can on the floor with a loud bang.

"I'm afraid the room is messier than usual, Ed. My last class was working on collages and we cleaned things up as best we could," explains Ms. Chow.

"Well, you didn't do a very good job and the next time I come in here and see the room like this, I'm just going to refuse to clean it," Ed says irritably.

Ms. Chow does not reply to his angry comment and realizes now that Mr. Parker is upset. After a few minutes of silence she takes a deep breath and says, "It's very clear that you are angry because my classroom needs more cleaning than usual, and I'm sorry you are so upset. But I make every effort to keep this room in good order and that's not always easy since it houses over one hundred-forty active young people throughout the day. And you know that most of the time you have very little cleaning to do in this room, so when you do, I don't expect you to give me a hard time about it."

"Hey! It's really no big thing!" remarks the startled custodian. "It's just that we're short-handed this afternoon and I've got ten extra rooms to clean before quitting time. So I got a little upset when I came in here and saw all this mess, but don't worry about it, Ms. C., because I didn't really mean I wouldn't clean your room if it was messy."

"Well, I'm sorry you've got to pull double-duty today, Ed, and that the condition of my classroom disappointed you, but I know you'll try your best to get everything done because you always do."

Analyzing the Communication Process

Special Considerations

It's usually best, at least initially, to address most concerns and complaints about school support service workers directly to the worker involved. It is also important to cultivate a mutually respectful working relationship with these behind-the-scenes people.

Examining the Strategies

Ms. Chow does not respond immediately to Ed Parker's angry venting, but instead, remains silent and collects her thoughts. She then calmly and respectfully informs the custodian that she expects him to do his job. She also tells him that his conduct toward her was unwarranted and unacceptable. She accepts Ed Parker's indirect apology and explanation for his peevishness and ends the exchange with a positive and honest statement.

Hints and Reminders

When communicating with a crabby custodian:

- Listen carefully to the custodian's comments.
- Avoid becoming defensive or petulant.
- Explain your side of the story.
- Offer an apology if one is warranted.

Worries and Warnings

In some school districts, less-skilled school service jobs have a high level of staff turnover, which is often true when private contractors are hired to provide staffing for routine services. If you do not know the worker, and have not had an opportunity to develop some type of rapport with him or her, it is best to address your concern to the person's immediate supervisor or your administrator. Regardless of whether you know your school custodians, convey respect for them and the job they do by following these simple rules:

- Keep your classroom as neat and orderly as possible.
- Insist that your students, within the limits of their abilities, follow the assertive housekeeper's golden rule—if you mess it up, you clean it up.
- Follow the assertive housekeeper's golden rule yourself.
- Compliment your custodians when they do a good job.

Communicating Effectively With Overly Controlling People

Overly controlling people micromanage everything. They tell others what to do and how to do it, even when they can't do it very well themselves. Their compulsion to control often causes them to be overbearing and difficult. As a teacher you may encounter overly controlling people in the form of authoritarian administrators, excessively helpful parents, charmingly assertive colleagues, and stubborn school service workers. When you meet these forceful people, try using the following strategies to communicate effectively with them and to offset their efforts at control.

Be Sure Your Communications are Direct and Clear

Overcontrollers frequently mistake lack of assertiveness for weakness, so if you want them to take you seriously, you must not be too subtle when dealing with them. For example, while most of your colleagues would more than likely respond favorably to the indirect and politely subtle, "I'm really overwhelmed with this new curriculum project and don't know how I'm ever going to get it

STRATEGIES FOR COMMUNICATING EFFECTIVELY WITH OVERLY CONTROLLING PEOPLE

Overly controlling people view things only from their own perspectives and approach most of life's problems with a "my-solution-is-the-only-right-solution" attitude. Communicate effectively with overcontrollers by persistently conveying the message that your feelings, opinions, ideas, and solutions are important and must be taken seriously.

- Be direct and clear: state exactly what you will and will not do.
- Be prepared: be certain of the reason for a meeting or the information you wish to convey beforehand.
- Be assertive: voice your opinion when it is called for and don't agree to decisions with which you are uncomfortable. If the person who is overly controlling is your supervisor or administrator, politely state your disagreement for the record.
- Be smart: whenever possible, use the overcontroller's talents at controlling to get things accomplished.

completed on time," by asking what they might do to help, controlling colleagues, in most instances, would not consider assisting you unless you assertively asked them to do so by stating, "I must have your help in order to complete this project on time."

Always be Well Prepared *Before* the Meeting

Since overcontrollers often present their suggestions and concerns in a forceful and highly confident manner, it is wise to be well prepared *before* meeting with them, especially when the meeting's purpose is to discuss job-related responsibilities. If an overcontroller insists on an impromptu meeting, sidestep the issue by unequivocally stating that you cannot meet at the present time but are agreeable to meeting at a time that is more mutually convenient. Also, do not allow a controlling person to manipulate you into agreeing in absentia to decisions made by others.

For example, an overly controlling teacher approaches Mr. Tactful, the chairperson of the school's special program committee, during lunch and tells him that the scheduled Tuesday afternoon committee meetings are very inconvenient for her. She says she has just spoken with two other committee members who agree that the Tuesday meetings are also inconvenient for them, and informs him that they all feel he should revise the schedule. Mr. Tactful refuses to be intimidated by Ms. Overly Controlling's forcefully assertive manner and politely replies that the current schedule was arranged by the entire committee during its last meeting and any revisions would have to be made by the committee during its next meeting.

Listen Carefully, But Don't Get Overwhelmed

When overcontrollers communicate with you, listen attentively to what they have to say, but don't allow the assertive manner in which they say it overwhelm you into agreeing to something that you don't believe is right. If you find them monopolizing the communication, politely but firmly interject your comments. You might say, for example, "I'm sorry, Allen, but I absolutely must break into this discussion," or "Excuse me for interrupting, but there's an important point you've overlooked."

When You Disagree, Don't Hesitate to Tell Them So

Overcontrollers often communicate their suggestions in an authoritative style that seems to negate the chance for disagreement. If you disagree with an overcontroller, however, don't let her authoritarian manner intimidate you. Gather your courage, look her in the eye and politely tell her you disagree. For example, you could say, "I'm afraid I can't agree with you, Jacinth. I just don't think it's a good idea for the Honor Society to hold an outdoor car wash in January." If the controlling person disregards or downplays your valid criticism or concern, be sure to reiterate your misgivings and stand firm when stating them.

If All Else Fails, Tactfully Pull Rank

It's not unusual for overcontrollers to browbeat others into accepting their suggestions, agreeing with their complaints, and supporting their solutions, even when such acceptance is ill-advised. If you are in a position to do so, pull rank on them and state the plan in your own words. You might say, "As chairman of the Faculty Social Committee, I totally oppose using Social Committee funds to pay for new carpeting for the guidance counselor's office and strongly suggest that we have the entire faculty vote on the issue."

If the controlling person ranks above you in the chain of command, respectfully voice your dissent by making a comment such as, "I realize I'm in the minority here, but I have to say that I disagree with the plan to implement the new reading curriculum without discussing it with the parents first."

Play to Their Strengths to Get Things Done

The path of least resistance when dealing with overcontrollers is to let them be in control whenever possible. Therefore, if you want their help implementing a suggestion or action plan, have them formulate several suggestions. You can then choose the one closest to your plan and work with them to revise it until it agrees with yours. For example, if you want 3,000 folding chairs set up in the school cafeteria, you could say to the controlling person, "I know you've been asked to set up the chairs for tomorrow's Parents Helping Parents outreach group. I need a way to set up the chairs so that everyone can meet in small groups of about ten, but can easily direct their attention to the podium at the front of the cafeteria. Do you have any ideas?" When you've asked for the overcontroller's opinion, the two of you can work together toward a plan that optimizes both of your ideas.

The Strategies at Work:
The Authoritarian Administrator

The teachers on the Woodhome Heights High School Curriculum Improvement Committee are meeting with the school principal, Mr. Winestadt, to devise a plan to improve the school's outdated technology curriculum. As they begin the meeting, Mr. Winestadt distributes papers to them and says, "I thought I'd do you folks a favor and save you some time. In front of you, you have a copy of the technology curriculum taught at my niece's school in California. I looked it over, and it seems pretty good to me, so if it's all right with everyone here, I think we should implement this program, giving credit to my niece's school district, of course."

When Mr. Weinstedt finishes, the committee members sit silently, nervously thumbing through the pages before them. After a minute or so, the committee chairperson, Mrs. Keaton, begins speaking. She looks directly at Mr. Weinstedt and addresses him calmly and evenly.

"Mr. Weinstedt, as the chairperson of this committee, I don't feel comfortable agreeing to a new technology curriculum that my committee hasn't had a chance to review, and I believe most of my fellow committee members agree."

She looks around the conference table before continuing and sees committee members nodding their heads in agreement.

"The purpose of this committee is to pool a variety of ideas so we can come up with the best possible technology curriculum to specifically meet the needs of Woodhome Heights students. I don't think it's best for us to implement another district's curriculum unless it is a good match for our students and we won't know that unless we take the time to thoroughly review your proposal."

"Well, if that's what you want to do, it's fine with me. I was just trying to save everyone some time, but if you all want to spend your afternoons meeting, it's okay with me. Just be sure you have your curriculum recommendations on my desk by the March fourth deadline!"

Analyzing the Communication Process

Special Considerations

Authoritarian administrators have a dictatorial leadership style. Most feel they have earned a position of authority because of their superior knowledge and judgment; they view collaboration with their staff as an unnecessary waste of time.

Communicating with authoritarian administrators requires maturity, confidence, and determination. You must be mature enough to stay calm and focused when approached in an extremely direct and assertive manner, confident enough to voice and defend your professional opinions, and determined enough to tactfully insist that your input be given careful consideration.

Examining the Strategies

The committee chairperson, Mrs. Keaton, listens attentively to Mr. Weinstadt's suggestion. She observes that her committee members agree with her and are uncomfortable with their administrator's "suggestion" of simply picking up someone else's curriculum. She musters her courage, looks directly at Mr. Weinstadt, and calmly and clearly states her case, stressing that it is the responsibility of her committee to place the best interests of Woodhome Heights students first.

Hints and Reminders

If you must communicate assertively with an authoritarian administrator:

- Don't make emotionally charged or accusatory comments, addressing the "fairness" of a situation. Don't completely reject the idea at first glance or suggest that it's "bad" or "stupid" or "wrong."
- Do make eye contact at various times throughout the conversation.
- Do speak assertively, but not disrespectfully, and make your

assertion a positive, rather than a negative one. Mrs. Keaton says to her administrator, "I don't think it's best for us to implement another district's curriculum . . ." She does not say, "I think it's a bad idea for us to pirate another school district's technology curriculum."

- Do stress that addressing your concern will improve the overall learning environment in your school. Mrs. Keaton says, for example, "The purpose of this committee is to pool a variety of ideas so we can come up with the best possible technology curriculum to specifically meet the needs of Woodhome Heights students."

Worries and Warnings

It's always important to document any official communications you have with your administrators, but this is especially so with authoritarian administrators. Often these overcontrollers will work well with others only when they know their comments and suggestions are being documented and might possibly find their way to higher authorities.

The Strategies at Work:
The Overly Helpful Parent

Miss Marx is working with her third-grade class to help them understand the concept that a fraction is an equal part of a whole object. The students are just beginning to get the idea when there is a knock at the door and a voice calls, "Hello! Anybody home?"

Miss Marx groans quietly as Mrs. White, a parent who volunteers at the school, flings open the door and rushes into the classroom. She is carrying a cage holding three loud guinea pigs. "Hi, Sally! Oh, excuse me. I mean Miss Marx," she says as the students giggle. "I brought these guys from the pet shop. I think they'll be a great addition to the class Science Corner."

By now the least-controllable children have left their seats and are flocked around Mrs. White and the guinea pig cage.

"All right, everyone!" says Miss Marx sternly. "All of those people out of their seats have to the count of ten to be seated and quiet! One, two, three . . ."

The students scramble quickly back to their seats. Miss Marx then says, "Boys and girls, I know you are excited about the guinea pigs and it was very thoughtful of Mrs. White to buy them for us, but we can't keep them."

"Aw, why not?" asks the class in unison.

"Yes, I'd like to know the answer to that myself," adds Mrs. White.

"Our school district has a strict rule against keeping live animals in classrooms for longer than two days," explains Miss Marx. "That's

WHEN GOOD VOLUNTEERS GO BAD

Overly helpful parents who volunteer at a school for many years can get very upset when a newcomer expresses displeasure with their method of helpfulness. When you know you are dealing with overly helpful long-term volunteers, take extra pains to diplomatically explain to them how their actions are creating problems for your students and suggest alternative actions they might try instead. For example, an overly helpful long-term volunteer has celebrated each child's birthday by bringing to school a decorated birthday cake and serving it to the class on every child's birthday every year. Three of your students' birthdays fall on three consecutive days in the same week. You feel the birthday cake celebrations are creating too much of a distraction and must be scaled back. You sit down with your overly helpful cake-baking parent and explain your concerns, then suggest that the parent bring in only one cake each month to simultaneously celebrate all birthdays for that month. Summer birthdays can be recognized with one cake at an end-of-the-school-year party.

because animals can't go without food or water when school is closed for several days, and it's not fair to keep animals caged up without a chance to get out of their cages and get exercise. But even more importantly, some children are highly allergic to animal hair and become very sick from animals in their classrooms."

Miss Marx finishes her explanation, looks around the room at her disappointed students, and focuses on Mrs. White.

"Well, it looks like I made a mistake," Mrs. White says. "I guess I'm going to have to try to return these guys to the pet store where I bought them."

"I'm afraid so," remarks Miss Marx.

"And Sharon," Miss Marx says quietly to Mrs. White, "In the future, you should probably speak with me before you buy things for my class, but thank you for trying to help."

Analyzing the Communication Process

Special Considerations

Helpful parents are important ingredients to successful schools. However, parents who are "helpful" to the extreme can be a detriment to the workings of a school. Because overly helpful parents are usually unaware that their efforts to help are, in fact, not really helpful, it is up to the teacher to assertively and tactfully tell them so.

Examining the Strategies

Miss Marx communicates directly and clearly with both her students and Mrs. White. She tells them candidly that live animals cannot be kept at school and precisely delineates the reasons why. Since experience has taught her that maintaining live animals in a classroom for even a few days can be a huge responsibility and distraction, she does not even broach the idea of appeasing her students by allowing the pets to stay for even a day or two. She speaks quietly and directly to Mrs. White and informs the parent of her expectations regarding future purchases for her classroom.

Hints and Reminders

When communicating with overly helpful parents:

- Remember that most parents truly want to be helpful but simply don't understand how seemingly innocent actions might negatively impact a classroom. It is your job to inform them about this.

- When discussing the problem of overly helpful parents, be polite and low key, not overbearing and sanctimonious. Instead of saying, "I can't give my students all these chocolate bars, Mrs. Hershey! They'll put my kids on a sugar high for the rest of the day!" you might say, "I'm sorry, Mrs. Hershey. I know you meant well by bringing chocolate bars as a special treat, but I'm afraid all of this candy will get my kids a little too hyped-up. So instead of giving out these chocolate bars all at once, I think I'll give them out a few at a time as special rewards."

- Be sure to explain in a low-key manner exactly how their overly helpful behavior causes problems for your students. For example, "I know you really want to help Joshua get ready for the bus on time, Mrs. Keating, but because he needs to learn to get himself organized, I'm going to have to ask you to not help him for a few days."

Worries and Warnings

Some teachers, especially those working with younger students, find themselves in the challenging position of having several overly helpful parents in their classrooms each day. Under the guise of being interested and involved, these parents run interference for and keep watch over their children to the detriment of everyone else. They overwhelm the classroom with their presence, interfere with teacher-to-student and student-to-student interactions, and stifle their child's growth as a confident and independent person.

If you are new to a school, ask other teachers if overly helpful parents are a problem and if so, what procedures are employed for dealing with them. Then be prepared to review those procedures with parents early in the school year and to politely and assertively enforce them throughout the year.

GUIDELINES FOR PARENT INVOLVEMENT IN YOUR CLASSROOM

- Parents must notify the teacher at least one day before they wish to make an extended classroom visit.

- No more than *two* (decide on the number best suited to you and your students' needs) parents may be "visiting" at any time, except for special events and American Education Week Open House.

- Parents may not visit for longer than *90 minutes* (decide the amount of time you and your students can easily tolerate).

- If more than *two* parents wish to visit during the same time period, visiting parents will be selected by lottery. *(If you have a wealth of parents who wish to visit your classroom, you may want to draw up a visitation schedule.)*

- Parents must sign in at the front office and obtain a visitor pass *before* coming to the classroom.

- Parents may not visit the classroom from 9 to 11 a.m. This is uninterrupted instructional time for my students.

- Visiting parents are expected to be good role models for their children. They should not talk when the teacher is talking, do their children's schoolwork for them, or interfere when the teacher is disciplining their child.

The Strategies at Work:
The Charmingly Assertive Colleague

It's Amy Potter's planning period and she is busy organizing her materials for her afternoon classes. Bud Simms, the reading resource teacher, comes rushing into her room.

"Hi, Amy! I'm in a bit of a jam, and I was hoping the best new teacher at Morning Star High might be able to help me out," says the smiling Bud.

"Okay, if I can," replies Amy helpfully.

"You see, I was supposed to do some preliminary testing on this kid and have the report completed in time for tomorrow's big ARD team meeting. Well, it completely slipped my feeble mind until yesterday. So I reworked my yesterday's schedule and completed the testing on the kid, but now I have to do this copious report and I'm running out of time. So I thought, 'Where can I find time in my schedule to write this blasted thing?' And that's when I realized I was scheduled to work with you and your classes this afternoon. Knowing that you're the kind of conscientious teacher who plans well, I thought I might be able to persuade you to handle your afternoon classes by yourself for today, and I promise you I'll make up the time with you tomorrow."

Amy pauses for a minute to think through Bud's proposal and then looks him in the eye and responds coolly, "Well, Bud, I can certainly understand why you're upset. I'm sure writing a diagnostic report for ARD takes time and effort, but I planned all of my afternoon lessons based on the fact that you were going to be here to help, and I can't change them on such short notice."

"Yeah, I can see your point," says Bud somewhat dejectedly. "Oh, wait a minute, I think I have a solution. How about I get my teaching assistant to stand in for me? That way you'll have an extra pair of hands and I'll have the time to do my report."

"No, Bud, that's not really a solution. Many of my students have serious reading problems and they need help from an experienced and knowledgeable reading teacher, not from his teaching assistant. Besides, I don't understand why you can't write that report after school today or even tonight," states Amy.

"I can't write it this afternoon or this evening because I have an important engagement I must attend," counters Bud, his voice rising.

"Well, I'm sorry that you're stuck, Bud, but unless one of the bosses tells me otherwise, I'll expect you to be here to help my students for the afternoon as scheduled," replies Amy.

"Oh, all right! I'll be here, but in the future, whenever you need a favor, don't even think about asking me," says the angry Bud as he heads for the door.

"I'm sorry you feel that way, Bud, but please keep in mind that I'm not asking for you to do any favors, just your job," Amy responds to the quickly exiting Bud.

Analyzing the Communication Process

Special Considerations

Charmingly assertive colleagues are coworkers who can cajole and charm almost anyone into doing their work for them. If you don't want to spend your time and energy managing their responsibilities, you must refuse to do the bidding of these disguised overcontrollers through determination and consistently clear communication.

Examining the Strategies

Amy Potter listens politely to what her charmingly assertive colleague has to say. She pauses and thinks carefully before responding. She commiserates with Bud's plight, and then calmly explains to him why she cannot grant his request. When Bud refuses to accept Amy's decision and offers an alternate plan, Amy offers a reasoned explanation as to why that plan is unacceptable and stresses that her students need his experience and knowledge.

She also suggests that instead of taking her class time to write the report, he could easily write the report on his own time. She then ends the discussion by reiterating her expectation that Bud do his job.

Hints and Reminders

Charmingly assertive colleagues often use flattery and guilt to get others to do their bidding. When communicating with these skilled manipulators:

- Be direct and assertive.
- Refuse to allow them to flatter you into doing their jobs for them.
- If they ask for your help and you offer them an explanation as to why you cannot help them, be prepared for them to use some part of your explanation to reject your refusal.
- If you feel they are taking advantage of your better nature, politely tell them so and refuse to help them out again.

Worries and Warnings

Once charmingly assertive colleagues see you as a person who can easily be flattered into doing their work for them, they will constantly rely on you for help. When you stand up to these colleagues and refuse to take on their responsibilities, they often react either by guilelessly admitting that they were trying to manipulate you or by feigning anger and threatening never to be helpful to you ever again. In either case, once you've called their bluff, charmingly assertive colleagues usually follow through with their job responsibilities, as long as you make sure they do.

Communicating Effectively
With Apathetic People

Apathetic people are uninvolved and indifferent, and don't want to invest themselves in most tasks. A crisis on the part of others definitely does not constitute a crisis for them, even when it will, in fact, affect them in the long run. They often avoid anything that hints of extra work and tend to avoid deep-seated commitments. You will meet them as uninvolved parents, laissez-faire administrators, and unmotivated coworkers.

STRATEGIES FOR COMMUNICATING EFFECTIVELY WITH APATHETIC PEOPLE

Apathetic people lack motivation and will not complete certain tasks unless they feel compelled to do them. Try employing the following strategies when communicating with apathetic people, but keep in mind it is most difficult to motivate those people who refuse to be motivated.

- Schedule definite times to meet with them and insist that they follow through.

- Express your expectations for them clearly and assertively.

- Document all communications you have with them and send out copies to all significant parties.

- Whenever possible, formulate a contract explicitly stating their responsibilities and have them sign it.

- Make it clear to them why it is in their best interest to follow through.

Schedule Definite Times to Meet and Insist They Follow Through

Indifferent people generally respond more consistently when you set a definite time to meet with them as opposed to having them contact you to set up a meeting. It is definitely not a good idea to leave a message on their voice mail asking them to contact you. It is better to simply leave a message indicating you will call back at a later time. Once you do arrange to meet with them, pressure them into attending by sending email reminders, written notes, and phone messages. Should they not show up for the meeting, contact them by phone and hold a phone conference.

For example, you and several other teachers absolutely must meet with an apathetic parent to discuss her son's serious learning problems. You send home a note with the child (or by email) offering the parent one of several possible meeting dates. When you receive no response within a day or two, you contact the parent by phone and leave a message stating the importance of the meeting.

If the parent does not get back to you, call again at a time you are almost certain she is home (i.e., early in the morning or later in the evening), and if you do not get through at that time, call her at work or contact her through the third party listed on her son's emergency card.

Express Your Expectations Clearly and Assertively

Within the bounds of professionalism, tell indifferent people exactly what you expect them to do. For example, "It is imperative that you sign and return the paperwork giving the school psychologist permission to test Albert. If I don't have your written permission by Friday the psychologist won't be able to schedule Albert's testing until next fall, and we won't know how to best work with Albert until sometime next school year. I know you don't want to wait until next year to help your son."

Document All Communications and Send Out Copies to All Noteworthy Parties

It's always a good idea to document important communications, but it is especially so when dealing with apathetic people since they tend to rely on, "I didn't know," or, "I wasn't informed," as their excuse for not following through. By following up all verbal communication with written documentation and sending copies to all noteworthy parties, you render their "I-was-left-out-of-the-loop" excuse implausible.

SAMPLE MEMO DOCUMENTING A MEETING

To: Mary Keystone, Jim Watson, Tessa Wells, Nita Marshall, Rodney Kareem

From: Florence Forthright

Re: Meeting with Ms. Keystone

Ms. Keystone has agreed to meet with us next Wednesday 2/17 at 3:30 p.m. in room 222 to discuss concerns about Albert's educational progress. Please arrive on time.

Florence Forthright

Whenever Possible, Formulate a Contract Stating Their Responsibilities and Have Them Sign It

It is fairly easy to convince apathetic people to sign a contract explicitly stating their responsibilities, since they usually see this as an easy way to end an unpleasant meeting. The difficult part is getting them to follow through. By delineating their responsibilities in writing, however, you draw their attention to those responsibilities and compel them to consider following through.

A contract for a parent would state everyone's responsibilities, not just those of the parent. For example, the contract for Ms.

Keystone, Albert's apathetic mother, might state that she would carefully review and sign all paperwork pertaining to Albert's educational evaluations, meet with the school psychologist to review the results of Albert's evaluations, and attend all meetings concerning Albert's academic progress. It would also state that the school psychologist would evaluate Albert on March 1 and review the results with Albert's mother on March 22, and Albert's teachers would devise an educational plan for Albert and share it with Ms. Keystone by April 1.

Explain to Them Why It Is in Their Best Interest to Get Involved

While it is difficult to motivate indifferent people to make a commitment and get involved, you can sometimes achieve this goal by explaining to them why doing so is in their best interest. You might, for example, tell Albert's mother that further testing will provide information to help Albert do better in school, and if he does better in school, Ms. Keystone won't have to be in as frequent contact with the school.

The Strategies at Work: The Laissez-Faire Administrator

Mrs. Abukutu, the drama and fine arts teacher at Maple Estates High School, is meeting with Mr. Esterson, the school principal, regarding her plans for the school's annual drama production.

"Thank you for following through on your commitment to meet with me, Mr. Esterson. I'm sorry I couldn't agree to reschedule this meeting as you wanted me to, but I'm afraid if I wait too much longer for your decisions on the content and format of this year's play, the drama club won't have enough time to deliver a high-quality production," explains Mrs. Abukutu. "I've prepared a copy of the play the drama club wants to perform, a schedule of the proposed performance dates, a draft of three

possible promotional announcements, and a list of local businesses that usually buy advertising in the playbill."

"Well, Mrs. Abukutu, this is quite impressive. You really have everything well organized."

"Thank you, Mr. Esterson," Mrs. Abukutu replies smiling. "Now, before I can proceed with the production, I need your permission to do so."

"Well, that's not a problem," replies Mr. Esterson. "You have it. Go ahead with your production."

"Are you sure you don't want to review the materials I've given you before signing off on this project?" questions the surprised Mrs. Abukutu.

"Why? Is there something wrong with your proposal?" counters Mr. Esterson.

"No, I don't believe so," replies Mrs. Abukutu. "But before I leave, Mr. Esterson," she continues assertively, "I'd like to have your written permission to take the necessary steps to produce this play."

"I told you to go ahead, Mrs. Abukutu. You don't need anything in writing."

"Yes, Mr. Esterson, I'm afraid I do. If for some reason you should be absent for an extended period of time, or someone objects to the play's content, or there's a problem with the logistics, I'll need documentation that I have your permission to produce this play and solve any problems associated with it."

"Well, my dear, I think you're being just a bit pessimistic, but if it'll make you happy, I'll have my assistant write something up, just so you have your documentation," Mr. Esterson replies amiably.

"Actually, Mr. Esterson, I already prepared something. It's in that packet of information I gave you. I think it's the last page or so," states Mrs. Abukutu a bit nervously.

The principal thumbs quickly through the pages and focuses on the last one in the packet. There is a long silence as he peruses the document. When he finishes, he takes a pen from his desk, signs the paper, and thrusts it at Mrs. Abukutu. "There you are, my dear. Now you have your documentation," he says somewhat resentfully.

TIPS FOR COMMUNICATING WITH LAISSEZ-FAIRE ADMINISTRATORS

- Arrange for a definite appointment time and, if at all possible, resist efforts on the part of your administrator to postpone your appointment.
- Be certain of your goals and priorities before the meeting.
- Stick to the topic at hand and resist being drawn into unrelated verbal asides.
- Take notes during the meeting and review them with your administrator at the meeting's end.
- Ask your administrator to put into writing any administrative duties she delegates to you. Should she refuse to do this, respectfully request that she delegate those duties to someone else.
- Keep documentation of everything you present to a laissez-faire administrator.

Analyzing the Communication Process

Special Considerations

Indifferent administrators demonstrate their indifference through their various leadership styles. These laissez-faire administrators demonstrate their indifference by soliciting lots of input, delegating lots of job responsibilities (even those that should not be delegated), and refusing to make decisions.

Obviously, it is not standard operating procedure for indifferent people to be hired as administrators. Generally speaking, only hard-working, truly dedicated people earn these positions. Over the course of time, however, the many demands and pressures of the job take their toll (just as they do with some teachers) and even some optimistic and dedicated administrators become jaded and indifferent.

Examining the Strategies

The high school drama teacher, Mrs. Abukutu, is thoroughly prepared for her meeting with her laissez-faire administrator, Mr. Esterson. Even before the meeting she demonstrates her assertiveness and determination by insisting that the meeting take place as scheduled. She also keeps Mr. Esterson focused on the topic

THE APATHETIC PERSON VS. THE PRIORITIZING PROCRASTINATOR

People in positions of authority with many responsibilities may, at times, appear to be apathetic when in fact they are simply prioritizing procrastinators. These harried people have so much to do and so little time in which to do it that they must always put off completing somewhat less-important tasks in favor of completing those that require immediate attention. Prioritizing procrastinators have learned that problems and required tasks of today will sometimes resolve themselves by tomorrow, such as when an irate parent who absolutely must speak with an administrator cools off overnight and thinks better of the idea by the next morning, or the administrative hierarchy rescinds a directive that an extensive student demographics report be completed by the end of the week. While prioritizing procrastinators are seldom ever apathetic, they can be just as frustrating to deal with, especially when your priorities are not their priorities. The strategies for communicating with apathetic people, however, are useful when trying to convince a prioritizing procrastinator that your concerns are important and need prompt attention.

at hand and prevents him from going off on verbal tangents. She presents him with the information he needs to make the necessary decisions regarding the drama club's performance. When Mr. Esterson gives his verbal consent to her proposal without reviewing it, she diplomatically reminds him that he might want to do so. She then presses him to give his written, as well as verbal, support for the project and, when he halfheartedly agrees to do so later, presents him with the materials so he can do so immediately.

Hints and Reminders

Laissez-faire administrators, in general, have an easy-going, non-confrontational leadership style. Those who are laissez-faire to the extreme place the majority of their responsibilities onto others and shirk blame when things go wrong.

Worries and Warnings

Since laissez-faire administrators usually appear to be genial and unassuming people, dealing with them assertively might seem disrespectful and insensitive. Bear in mind, however, that by compelling laissez-faire administrators to make, record, and stand by their decisions you are actually encouraging them to do a better job.

The Strategies at Work: The Uninvolved Parent

Mr. Hammond, a teacher at Rosa Parks Middle School, is speaking by phone with Marvin Boyd's father. Marvin is a student in Mr. Hammond's U.S. government class and Mr. Boyd is notorious for missing scheduled parent–teacher conferences and failing to return report cards, permission slips, and teachers' phone calls and email messages. Mr. Hammond has tried for several days to get in touch with Mr. Boyd and has finally reached him by phone early in the morning. He wants Mr. Boyd to sign and return a permission slip so Marvin can go on a much-anticipated field trip with his class.

"Mr. Boyd, my U.S. government class is taking a field trip to Washington, D.C. in two weeks and I know Marvin wants to go, but he can't unless you sign and return his trip permission slip by the end of this week," says Mr. Hammond.

"Really?" replies Mr. Boyd. "Marvin never said anything to me about a trip to D.C., and I never saw a trip permission slip."

"I'm not sure why you haven't heard about the trip," says Mr. Hammond. "The class has held several fundraisers to pay for it and three written notices were sent out about it. In any case, my students are looking forward to this trip and as of right now, Marvin is the only one who can't go because I don't have your permission for him to do so."

"Well, come to think of it, I do remember seeing some stuff about a trip, but, it seems to me, the price was just a little too steep for my budget," says Mr. Boyd.

"But Mr. Boyd, the bus fare and entrance fees are paid for. That's why the kids did all those fundraising activities, so everyone could afford to go on this trip. If Marvin wants to buy a lunch or souvenirs, he'll need some extra cash for those things, but otherwise, the trip is free."

"So it won't cost me anything to let Marv go on this trip?" queries Mr. Boyd.

"That's right, and I'm certain Marvin will be a very appreciative young man if you sign off on this trip," comments Mr. Hammond.

"Well, I never said he couldn't go. I just didn't know anything about it 'til right now. It's okay with me if he goes on the trip as long as it doesn't cost me anything, and besides it'll probably be a good thing if it makes him a little less moody," says Mr. Boyd.

"Great," replies Mr. Hammond, "I'll expect to see that signed permission slip tomorrow morning."

"I don't know about that," cautions Mr. Boyd. "I don't have a permission slip to sign."

"Not a problem," replies Mr. Hammond. *"I gave an extra trip permission notice to Marvin. Just tell him you want to sign it, and I'm sure he'll have no trouble finding it."*

Analyzing The Communication Process

Special Considerations

Since parents must be informed of their children's educational progress and must grant permission for them to participate in such special school programs as field trips, sporting events, after school clubs, and diagnostic testing, communication between teachers and parents is always warranted. However, the task of keeping disinterested parents informed and involved can be especially frustrating and time-consuming for busy teachers. The secret to establishing effective communication with these seemingly indifferent individuals is to appeal to their inherent self-interest. You must explain to them in great detail how they, not necessarily their children, have the most to gain from getting involved, if only temporarily. It also means that since there can be serious underlying reasons for these parents' apparent disinterest in their children's education (such as family health issues, financial difficulties, or emotional problems), you must make every effort to avoid approaching them in a disrespectful and judgmental manner. Not only is such behavior on the part of a teacher unprofessional, it also negates any possibility of cooperation from uninvolved parents.

Examining the Strategies

Mr. Hammond begins his communication with Mr. Boyd by clearly stating the purpose for his call. He stresses that attending the trip is important to Mr. Boyd's son, Marvin, and that Marvin is the only student without parental permission to go on the field trip. When Mr. Boyd says he didn't know about the trip, Mr. Hammond gently contradicts him by recounting the many ways Mr. Boyd could have learned about it. When the father eventually admits he may have seen some information about the trip, Mr. Hammond makes no so-I-was-right-after-all comments, and when Mr. Boyd attempts to use the trip's cost to legitimize his inaction, the teacher informs him that the trip is virtually cost free. (If there had been a cost for the trip, Mr. Hammond would have arranged for Marvin's fees to be paid out of school discretionary funds prior to speaking with the father.) Finally, when Mr. Boyd agrees to sign off on the trip but doesn't have the necessary permission slip, Mr. Hammond is prepared and tells him to check with Marvin who has the trip permission slip Mr. Hammond has given him ready and waiting.

Hints and Reminders

When communicating with uninvolved parents:

- Persistently (but politely) attempt to contact them until you actually get in touch with them.
- Stay upbeat and positive.
- Gently and good naturedly refute their arguments and excuses for not getting involved.
- Refuse to let their negativity or lack of concern affect you.
- Detail the ways their involvement can benefit them personally.

Worries and Warnings

Some uninvolved parents can have serious social or emotional problems that can severely impact the health and well being of their children. If you suspect that this is the case with a particular parent, you must inform the appropriate authorities (in most cases your school's administrator, guidance counselor, and social worker) so they can take the necessary steps to protect the child from further harm.

Also, cultural differences and language barriers can sometimes cause parents to appear unconcerned about their child's education when this is not the case. Once you establish communication with parents and realize that they are not apathetic but view their parenting role from a different cultural perspective or are struggling to master a new language, your dealings with them should be more moderate.

The Strategies at Work: The Indifferent Colleague

It's Wayne Copeland's planning period and he and Marlin Allen are meeting to plan a health unit they must teach as a team.

"Hey, Wayne, how's it going?" says Marlin as he enters the room carrying a cup of coffee and munching a donut.

"It's going okay," replies Wayne, plopping a thick lesson plan folder on his desk. "Did you bring your plans?"

"Oh, man! I knew I forgot something," replies Marlin as he heads for the door. He leaves and returns ten minutes later empty-handed. "Hey, man, you know, I think I'm losing it. I looked everywhere and I just can't find those plans. I think I must have left them at home. Let's just work from your stuff and I'll add my piece later," he suggests as he heads for the door.

"Now where are you going?" asks Wayne his voice rising in frustration.

"Just chill, will you? I gotta make a pit stop," replies Marlin.

"Wait a minute, man," demands Wayne. "Before you leave again we need to get a few things straight. I'm willing to work with you on this unit as long as you're willing to do your share, but so far, from where I'm standing, you haven't done very much except waste time."

"Aw, come on now. Don't tell me you're going to make a big stink just because I forgot some plans and have to visit the men's room," says Marlin shaking his head in disbelief.

"Yes, I'm afraid I am," retorts Wayne. "You know it's not just about your forgetting the plans and having to use the restroom. It's about wasting my time and not seeming to care about getting the job done.

And if this were the first time you were late and unprepared, I would take it in stride, but this is the third time it has happened. So I'm going to schedule another meeting with you, Marlin, but this time I'm going to put it in the form of an official memo and send copies to our department chair, our administrators, and our supervisor. If you don't show or you're unprepared, I'll send them copies of the minutes of the meeting that will inform them of what's not happening and schedule a follow-up meeting with them and the two of us to explain why we aren't completing our assigned planning."

Analyzing the Communication Process

Special Considerations

Encouraging indifferent teachers to do their jobs is a difficult task that requires perseverance, directness, and, at times, even coercion. As a result, highly motivated teachers usually just give up and do their less-motivated colleagues' work for them. This assures that the work actually gets done in a timely and effective fashion, but, sadly, it only encourages their colleagues' lazy behavior. Therefore, if you don't want to do others' work in addition to your own, you must not allow them to procrastinate and circumvent their part of your shared responsibilities.

Examining the Strategies

Wayne is frustrated with his colleague's relaxed attitude, and conveys that message clearly and assertively to Marlin. He tells Marlin he will no longer tolerate his procrastination and lack of involvement and then informs him of exactly what he will do if Marlin ignores his responsibilities again.

Hints and Reminders

Because usually you will have no real authority over your fellow teachers, you must rely upon either finesse or coercion to encourage them to follow through on their commitments to you. While finesse works with most colleagues, those who are seriously disengaged and totally uncommitted require more coercive measures. When communicating with apathetic colleagues:

- Inform them clearly and unequivocally of your expectations. Take care not to falter because you are a sensitive and conscientious person.

- Document your efforts to encourage an indifferent colleague to follow through; also document the excuses he or she makes for not doing so.

- Send copies of your documentation to all involved parties, including your lax colleague.

- As a last alternative, arrange a meeting with you, your colleague, and an administrator to discuss the problem.

Worries and Warnings

Sometimes because of personal problems such as family illness, serious financial troubles, the challenges of parenting, or matrimonial difficulties, fellow teachers might appear indifferent to their job responsibilities when in fact they are not. Therefore, don't assume whenever colleagues miss a scheduled meeting or fail to complete their part of a project on time that they are slackers, but instead give them the benefit of the doubt until they prove otherwise.

Communicating Effectively With Anxious People

Anxious people are excessively fearful people. They may be overly protective parents who want to shield their children not only from danger, but also from life's inevitable disappointments and failures. Perhaps they are indecisive administrators reluctant to make unpopular decisions, or insecure colleagues in constant fear of displeasing the powers that be.

STRATEGIES FOR COMMUNICATING EFFECTIVELY WITH ANXIOUS PEOPLE

Anxious people are the world's worrywarts. They firmly believe in Murphy's Law, expect things to always go wrong, and if at all possible, avoid taking any kind of risk. To communicate effectively with anxious people:

- Think about concerns they may present and prepare positive, reassuring responses before meeting with them.

- When arranging a meeting, inform them well in advance of the meeting's agenda.

- During the meeting, avoid surprises and follow the pre-planned agenda as closely as possible.

- Highlight several preventive aspects or positive benefits of your proposals.

- Carefully explain plans for managing problems and emergencies.

- Inform them as quickly and calmly as possible when things do go wrong or when there is an emergency.

Prepare Positive and Reassuring Responses

To establish effective communication with anxious people, you must convince them that you are a reliable person who understands and is responsive to their concerns. Do this by imagining their concerns before you communicate with them and by preparing logical and reassuring responses to them.

For example, if you must work with an anxious colleague on a staff development presentation, you would anticipate that he or she would be worried to the extreme about such things as not having enough time to complete the project, exactly what material to include, and how well the presentation will be received. You would then prepare a tentative timeline for the project, jot down a few ideas about what might be included, and think of a few comments you might make to reassure your colleague that the presentation will be well received. Try comments such as, "You've done several staff development presentations in the past, and they've always been helpful. This one will be too," or "If we do a good job of preparing and give the staff pertinent information, they can't help but like our presentation."

Share a Meeting's Agenda Well in Advance

Since anxious people generally are much more at ease when they know what to expect, it's usually a good idea to inform them of a meeting's proposed agenda well in advance of the meeting. The problem with employing this strategy is that once they know the agenda, they have additional time to ponder the topics and suggest difficulties.

Avoid Surprises During a Meeting and Follow the Pre-planned Agenda as Closely as Possible

Stick to the agenda and avoid surprises. This will help reduce stress levels and allow anxious people to be more receptive to the discussion at hand. Plan to begin and end meetings with positive, easily managed topics and plan to tackle the more unpleasant, less-easily managed topics at some point between the positives.

Highlight Several Preventive Aspects or Positive Benefits of Your Proposals

Since anxious people have a tendency to view anything new or different with pessimism, explain to them the preventive aspects or positive benefits of your plans. For example, if an overly protective parent views your school's annual Sports Day as harmful to her child because she might suffer from heat stroke or sun poisoning, you could assure the parent of the following: all activities from 12 to 2 p.m. take place inside the air-conditioned school, children are encouraged to wear sunscreen, children are given frequent drink breaks, and those who appear to be overheated are required to take cool-down breaks.

Carefully Explain Plans for Managing Problems and Emergencies

Attempt to calm the pessimistic fears of anxious people by carefully explaining your plans for managing problems and emergencies. However, be prepared for them to suggest additional concerns and contingencies that have not occurred to you. If you cannot immediately think of viable solutions for these newly presented problems, ask the anxious person to suggest possible solutions.

Inform Anxious People as Quickly and Calmly as Possible When Things Go Wrong

Keeping the trust and confidence of anxious people is essential to continuing productive communications with them, so inform them as quickly and calmly as possible when unforeseen problems arise. If, for example, a disgruntled parent declares that he is going to call local television stations to report the sad state of your school's library and you cannot diplomatically convince him that doing so would harm the school's image, it is important that you quickly inform your anxious administrator of the parent's intentions.

The Strategies at Work:
The Overly Protective Parent

Mr. Collins, a science teacher at Sandburg Middle School, is meeting with Mrs. Gershwin, the mother of one of his sixth-grade students.

"Mr. Collins, I asked to meet with you because I'm concerned about this field trip you've planned for my daughter's class to the Franklin Institute in Philadelphia."

"All right, Mrs. Gershwin," replies Mr. Collins evenly. "Tell me what concerns you have."

"Well, for one thing, you're using the Arcadia Bus Company, and have you seen the buses they use? They look like rent-a-wrecks! For another thing, I don't think you have enough chaperones to monitor a class of 36 kids. How many chaperones do you have, anyway? Also, what in the world are all those kids going to do for lunch and dinner, and where are they going to rest if they get tired? Speaking of which, don't you think a two-and-a-half-hour bus ride each way is a bit much for these kids? That's five hours on a bus! Plus everyone has to be here at Sandburg by 6:30 a.m. and they won't get back to school until 8:30 p.m. just so they can wander around the streets of Philadelphia and ride the dangerous subway!" Mrs. Gershwin expounds.

"I just think this whole trip is a bad idea, but you've convinced my daughter that it's the trip of her lifetime and now I don't know what to do. If I don't let her go, I'll be the bad guy and she'll pout around the house for days on end, but if I do let her go and something happens to her, I'll never forgive myself. I told her I thought maybe I'd volunteer to go along as a chaperone, but she threw a fit and said she didn't want her mommy going with her to hold her hand."

Mr. Collins listens patiently as Mrs. Gershwin relates her concerns, frustrations, and fears and then says, "You have some valid concerns, Mrs. Gershwin, but I believe I have addressed most of them in planning for this trip. The bus company will transport my class in a brand-new bus and my research indicates that the Arcadia Bus Company has an excellent safety record. There are six chaperones going on the trip in addition to me and my teaching assistant.

"We will stop for lunch at a cafeteria near the Institute and stop at a roadside restaurant for dinner. The kids will be under close supervision when traveling the Philadelphia streets and subway. Each of the chaperones will have a cell phone, so if we do get separated or there is an emergency, we can be in touch.

"As far as your concerns about the long bus trip and long day go: yes, the day and bus ride are long, but probably no longer than a lot of these kids experience on vacation trips with their families, only this time they'll be traveling with their school family," Mr. Collins says, concluding his explanation.

"Well, I guess that's it then," replies a resigned Mrs. Gershwin. "From what you've said, I suppose it's okay for Jennine to go on this trip, but I sure do wish it was closer to home!"

Analyzing the Communication Process

Special Considerations

Communicating effectively with overly protective parents requires patience, understanding, self-control, and an arsenal of reassuring responses. Be prepared to demonstrate that your decisions and deeds are predicated on ensuring their child's safety and welfare.

Examining the Strategies

Having learned from his teaching colleagues that Mrs. Gershwin "tends to be a worrywart," Mr. Collins is prepared to respond to and refute many objections and concerns regarding the class field trip. He listens graciously as Mrs. Gershwin presents an extensive list of complaints and concerns. He then calmly diminishes those concerns about the trip by explaining that the bus company has an excellent safety record, there are more than enough chaperones, lunch and dinner accommodations are planned, and means of communication in case of an emergency are in place.

Hints and Reminders

Overly protective parents need reassurance that their children are safe and secure, and are most receptive to communication from teachers who provide them with such reassurance. Communicate effectively with overly protective parents by:

- Preparing responses to their potential concerns before communicating with them.
- Listening patiently and empathetically when they express their concerns.
- Explaining in detail how your current plans and actions already address their concerns.
- Accepting workable and sound suggestions from them.

Worries and Warnings

Once you win their trust, you might find that some overly protective parents view you as their own personal sounding board and complaint department, which can drain you of your time and energy. When they contact you with a complaint or anecdotal story, explain to them that your time is limited (You might say, "Mrs. Gershwin, I'm afraid I only have ten minutes for this call"), listen politely to their comments, and end the call. Don't allow them to drag you into a lengthy conversation that simply affords them the opportunity to vent.

The Strategies at Work: The Indecisive Administrator

Mrs. Ridley, the art department chairperson at Abe Lincoln High School, is meeting with her principal, Dr. Michaels, to discuss a proposal to purchase a new kiln for the art department.

"Thanks for meeting with me, Dr. Michaels," she begins.

"No thanks necessary, Mrs. Ridley. Meeting with staff members is part of my job," he replies.

"Dr. Michaels, as you know from the memo I sent you, I'm very concerned about the antiquated kiln we're using in the art department, and I need your written permission to purchase a new one," Mrs. Ridley explains.

"Yes, I read your memo, and while your assessment of the condition of the art department's kiln is most likely correct, I think it would be best if I appointed a committee of three or four teachers to do some research on the matter," states Dr. Michaels.

Mrs. Ridley takes a deep breath and collects her thoughts. She knows that Dr. Michaels is often hesitant to make even the most mundane decision unilaterally and wants to convince him to sign off on the kiln purchase during this meeting.

"Dr. Michaels," she begins, "while I think it's usually a good idea to get input from others before making a major purchase, I can assure you that the only teachers on your staff who know or care anything about purchasing kilns are the art teachers, and we all agree that the old kiln is borderline dangerous. Its electric elements are brittle and its outer casing is cracked. We've researched the best makes and models for the school's needs, received permission from the district art supervisor for the purchase, and have the funds in the art budget. We simply need your written permission to go ahead. Also, Dr. Michaels, it's nearly the end of the first semester and with everyone busy closing out grades and preparing report cards, teachers aren't going to be very pleased with being asked to serve on a kiln committee."

"Well, Mrs. Ridley, put that way, I can see what you mean." Dr. Michaels glances over the purchase voucher that Mrs. Ridley has handed him. "You're sure you have the art supervisor's backing on this and you've done all the necessary research?"

"Yes sir, I can assure you we have," replies Mrs. Ridley confidently.

"All right, then. Go ahead and order the thing," he says as he signs the purchase voucher.

Analyzing the Communication Process

Special Considerations

Because indecisive administrators have difficulty making even commonplace decisions without wavering and waffling, communicating effectively with them requires teachers to be prepared to assertively and respectfully present their points of view and defend their proposals. It's important when you meet with an indecisive administrator regarding the resolution of an issue that you strongly encourage him or her to make a decision on that issue during your meeting.

Examining the Strategies

Mrs. Ridley requests a meeting with Dr. Michaels by memo. Knowing that Dr. Michaels is uncomfortable making decisions and often postpones them, she attends the meeting with information to help him make an immediate decision. When Dr. Michaels suggests appointing a committee to study the proposal, Mrs. Ridley calmly explains several reasons why this is unnecessary. She then tells Dr. Michaels that her supervisor has agreed to the kiln purchase and the funding is available. This information provides Dr. Michaels with further reasons to make an affirmative decision regarding Mrs. Ridley's request.

Hints and Reminders

When communicating with indecisive administrators:

- Present as much information as possible to support your position.

- Invite others who share your views to attend the meeting (be sure your administrator agrees to this prior to the meeting) or present evidence that others agree with your position.

- Agree to take responsibility for implementing an action plan to achieve your goals. (Do this only if you have the support of other staff members or you are highly dedicated to achieving your goals.)

- Take notes during your meeting, review them with your administrator, and share them with all concerned parties.

- If at all possible, assertively encourage your administrator to arrive at a decision before the meeting concludes.

Worries and Warnings

Since indecisive administrators can become even more so when they feel they are being pressured into making decisions, it is best not to be forceful or confrontational when communicating with them.

The Strategies at Work: The Insecure Colleague

It's the end of the school day and Melanie Adams is heading to the faculty room for a soda when Missy Mendenhal, another teacher at the school, stops her.

"Oh, Melanie, I'm so glad I caught you. I need your advice on that lesson I'm planning to teach when Mrs. Ward comes in to evaluate me," says Missy anxiously.

"Okay, Missy, but I'm not so sure my advice will be all that helpful," replies Melanie with a sigh. Missy has constantly asked Melanie for advice during the first few weeks of school and Melanie doesn't want her to depend on her throughout the entire year.

"Sure it will," counters Missy. "You always know what you're doing and your lessons always work out."

"That's what you think," replies Melanie. "There are many times when I have my doubts about what I'm doing, and lots of times when my lessons don't work out the way I plan them."

"Really?" says Missy incredulously. "But it's easy for you. You never seem to struggle the way I do."

"Listen, Missy," states Melanie, *"All I do is plan and then try to teach lessons that help my students learn the curriculum. I feel that as long as my students are learning, I'm doing my job and there's little reason for anyone to have a serious complaint. I'll be glad to set aside a half hour each week for the next month to go over your lessons with you and suggest some possible teaching strategies. After that month, though, I won't help you as much because I'll expect you to have enough confidence to plan and teach your lessons without my help."*

Analyzing the Communication Process

Special Considerations

Teachers instinctively want to help other teachers, and this can become a problem when those in need of help are very insecure. Teachers who seriously lack self-confidence can easily become overly dependent on others for support, guidance, lesson plans, and even classroom discipline.

Examining the Strategies

Melanie Adams is concerned about Missy Mendenhal's over-dependence on her. When Missy catches Melanie after school and doesn't request her help but instead demands it, Melanie decides to set some limits with her insecure colleague. Melanie tries to help Missy understand that although she strives to plan successful lessons, sometimes they aren't successful, just as Missy's aren't always successful. Melanie then agrees to help Missy but only for a clearly defined period of time.

Hints and Reminders

Bolster the confidence that insecure teachers have in their accomplishments and abilities and communicate effectively with them by:

- Being patient and understanding with them, yet insisting that they respect your time.

- Reminding them that all teachers face similar challenges and disappointments.

- Stressing their teaching strengths and successes.

- Instructing them to replicate their successes and learn from their failures.

- Setting guidelines for helping them that limit their dependence on you and lead them to become more self-reliant. For example, you might tell them that you'll come in and observe the class dynamics and suggest some strategies she might use to help her run her class more effectively.

Worries and Warnings

Regardless of your best efforts at helping insecure colleagues become more secure and self-reliant, some colleagues may still remain overly dependent on you for support. When this happens, be highly assertive and politely refuse to provide them with additional assistance. While refusing to help needy colleagues may seem harsh, it forces them to make some difficult decisions regarding their teaching careers.

Part IV
Communicating Under Duress

Relating unpleasant information to those most affected by it or communicating in a negative environment can be challenging for even the most capable communicator. However, there are some strategies you can use to help you convey bad news more effectively and to communicate in difficult circumstances.

Communicating Unpleasant Information

Since recipients of bad news are more receptive to hearing it when communicated by someone they trust, you must build that trust long before you have to convey unpleasant information to them. If you haven't established trust through past communication, follow the guidelines—but be prepared for an acrimonious encounter.

STRATEGIES FOR COMMUNICATING UNPLEASANT INFORMATION

- Be empathetic.
- Begin communication on a positive note.
- Present negative information tactfully.
- Address questions and concerns.
- Suggest ways you might resolve serious differences of opinion.

Be Empathetic

Put yourself in the other person's place and think about how you would best grasp particularly unpleasant news. For example, as a parent, how would you most appreciate being told that your child threw a lit firecracker into a school trash receptacle and caused an explosion "heard around the school?" Or how would you prefer to be told that extensive diagnostic testing indicates your child has a serious learning disability? Would you be more appreciative of a low-key, it's-not-the-end-of-the-world presentation, an all-business, just-the-facts presentation, or a highly confrontational, let's-play-the-blame-game presentation?

Begin Communication on a Positive Note

Regardless of how unpleasant the information is that you must share, strive to begin communicating on a positive note. Under the most trying of circumstances, you can always say, "I'm so glad you could speak with me about this problem on such short notice. I really appreciate your support."

Present Negative Information Tactfully

Remember that while the information you share may seem routine and only mildly upsetting to you, it may seem much worse to the recipient. Therefore, it's important to present negative information as diplomatically as possible, tailoring it to the sensibilities of its recipient. For example, if you must inform a sensitive teaching colleague that she has done a poor job of planning a lesson that you and she are team-teaching together, you should avoid bluntly stating, "I think you've done a poor job with this lesson," in favor of the more considerate, "This plan doesn't seem to meet the lesson's objectives."

Address Questions and Concerns

Address any questions and concerns the recipients of unpleasant information may have. When you cannot answer a question, tell them so and direct them to the people who can. Since people receiving bad news are often too upset to ask questions or express concerns, you should mention questions and concerns other people in similar situations have expressed and invite the person to contact you if they have additional questions.

Suggest Ways You Might Resolve Serious Differences of Opinion

It's not unusual for the recipients of unpleasant information to disagree with its validity. When this happens, suggest some ways this problem might be resolved, such as meeting with a neutral third party. You could also do additional fact finding, or take the problem to someone higher in the chain of command for an authoritative decision. For example, you might propose that a child who is failing your beginning algebra class enroll in a summer remedial math program. Her parents, however, might not see the need for their daughter "to give up her summer vacation," and reject your proposal. As a way to resolve your differing opinions, you might then suggest that the child take a diagnostic test to gauge her strengths and weaknesses in math. The diagnostic test will either verify your assessment, or give you a better understanding of the child's math skills.

Communicating Unpleasant Information to Parents

When communicating unpleasant information to parents, realize that you can easily provoke their protective instincts by making comments that they perceive as unfairly critical of their children. If you have communicated with them before, you will have some idea of how to speak to them so they do not become overly defensive and unreceptive. If you have had little contact with them, review the child's records before your meeting to determine if the parents were informed of this problem in the past, choose your initial comments with care, observe their reactions to them, and be prepared for the strong possibility that those comments will engender negative and unyielding responses.

Also, as you share unpleasant information with parents, understand that any unkind remarks they make are often the result of their protective instincts and not, in most cases, their actual feelings toward you as a person and teacher. For example, if you find yourself in the difficult position of informing parents that their child was caught cheating on a major test, they may defend their child, saying she was the victim of inaccurate observations, deliberately false accusations, overtaxing academic demands, or poor teaching.

Be Positive and Empathetic

Begin the communication process on a positive note by thanking the parents for coming, or if this is a telephone conference, for speaking with you. Then make a few genuine comments or general inquiries about them such as, "I heard the traffic is terrible tonight. I hope you didn't have too much trouble getting here," or "You know Mr. & Mrs. Jones, I think of you whenever I see that commercial for your furniture store on television. Is it true you are expanding to a larger store?"

REFUSE TO PLAY THE BLAME GAME

Because of their protective instincts, parents can easily become defensive when others criticize their children. This defensiveness often causes them to deny their child has a problem and sometimes leads them to blame others for the child's difficulties. When parents are in denial, patiently and tactfully present objective information such as diagnostic test results, work samples, and conduct reports to help them better understand their child's imperfections, and when they play the blame game, avoid becoming a participant.

Don't allow them to blame their child's poor performance or inappropriate behavior on others and tactfully refuse to listen to "he-said she-said" diatribes against the school district, the administration, the child's past and present teachers, and/or other children and their parents. When someone or something else is responsible for the child's problems (for example, a student clique, a physical handicap, a psychological problem, or a learning disability), acknowledge the fact and focus on what can be done to correct the situation. When the child's problems are of his or her own making, calmly, persistently, and tactfully refute the parents' defensive explanations, excuses, and irrelevant questions, and gently help them understand their child is the one at fault.

Such comments and inquiries, when not intrusive, indicate a personal interest in the parents, put them at ease, and sometimes lead to insights that can help you better tailor your forthcoming comments to their particular circumstances. The simple colloquial question, "How have you been doing?" can lead to the disclosure that a family member has suffered a serious health problem or the breadwinner has recently lost his or her job.

After you inquire about the parents, make some positive comments about the child. When possible, relate your comments in some way to your work with their child in the classroom. You

A middle school science teacher, Mr. Kirby, meets with parents to inform them that their child is performing poorly in his science class. They question why he has not met with them about the problem sooner. He calmly explains that it is his usual policy not to request a parent conference unless a student does poorly on two consecutive major tests. They then question the validity of the current science curriculum. Mr. Kirby patiently replies that the science curriculum was written by a team of highly experienced science educators with input from a panel of interested citizens. He then suggests that they might voice their concerns by becoming panel members.

Next the parents state that they believe their child would have a much better foundation in science if the small private elementary school she formerly attended had taught science as part of the daily curriculum. Mr. Kirby agrees that their daughter is missing some science basics but stresses that she can gain those basics with some extra effort and study. Finally, the parents suggest that their daughter would do much better in Mr. Kirby's science class if she did not have to sit next to Bobby Markam because Bobby has serious behavior problems and his inappropriate behavior distracts their daughter from concentrating on her science work. Mr. Kirby responds that, to date, none of the students in his science class have displayed serious behavior problems and there have been few, if any, distractions during class.

might say, for example, "Jake certainly has a wealth of determination. Once he makes up his mind to do something, he does it. We just have to help him make better decisions about when it's best to be determined and when it's not." If you cannot think of any positive comments relating to the child's efforts in your class, remark about his or her achievements in other classes or even accomplishments totally unrelated to school. You might say, for example, "I understand Marty scored the winning touchdown in Friday night's football game," or, "Mary Ann just told me that she earned her Lifeguard Certification and already has a part-time job offer from the Hopp Wright Inn."

Present Negative Information Diplomatically

Once everyone is somewhat more at ease and receptive, diplomatically introduce the actual purpose of the meeting. One way to do this is to use your initial positive comments to segue into unpleasant news. For example, "Unfortunately, Marty's wonderful exploits on the football field haven't been carrying over to his World History class. That's the main reason I wanted to speak with you; to see if together we could work out some sort of solution to help Marty improve his history grades, because if he doesn't do so soon, he may fail World History."

Address Questions and Concerns

After you introduce the unpleasant news, be prepared to answer the parents' questions and address their concerns. Marty's parents, for example, might want to know exactly what his grades are, when they started to plummet, what he can do to improve them, and what they can do to motivate him to improve them. They also might question why you didn't let them know about their son's falling grades more quickly and why students have to know a lot of meaningless dates in order to do well on a history exam.

How well you respond to parents' questions and concerns depends on how well prepared you are for the meeting and how calm and reasoned you remain during it. Since you already know the information you will present, anticipate parents' questions and concerns and prepare responses to them. Knowing you are prepared will give you an aura of confidence and help you stay calm.

Suggest Ways to Resolve Differences

If you and the parents cannot reach a mutually agreeable understanding or solution to a problem, suggest some viable ways you might resolve your differences. For example, Marty's parents may insist that you permit him to rewrite a failing research paper;

however, in adherence to your classroom standards, you refuse to allow him that privilege. You might then suggest that you and the parents meet with the school's history department chairperson and abide by her decision, or that Marty research and write an additional paper that could improve his history grade.

Communicating Unpleasant Information to Administrators

Communicating unpleasant information to administrators requires a slightly different approach than communicating negative information to parents. First, since administrators are busy people with many responsibilities, you must decide if the information actually must be shared with them. Is it best shared by memo, in person, or in a meeting with several others? On occasion, you must decide who is the appropriate administrator with whom to share the information.

Deciding What Information to Share

Ideally, administrators view themselves as the instructional leaders of their schools whose job it is to set high academic standards, mentor teachers, counsel students, and address the concerns of parents. In reality, however, most administrators today can do these things only peripherally, and actually spend the majority of their time addressing school safety and public relations concerns. Administrators need to know as quickly as possible that a student has a knife in her backpack, a strange man is loitering outside your classroom, one of your students accidentally took the wrong bus home, or a community activist parent sent you a note threatening to go to the media about the indecent illustrations used in the new sex education curriculum. In short, share any information with your administrators that might help them prevent future problems or allow them to be better prepared for dealing with them.

Deciding Where and How to Share Information

While you can share less-consequential information (such as reminders that a student cut your third-period Spanish class again) with administrators in public places such as in the halls or the faculty lounge, unpleasant information is best conveyed to them within the confines of their office. This not only allows for privacy but also gives them the opportunity to listen, uninterrupted, to the information that you share.

When the situation is not an emergency, write a note requesting a meeting with your administrator. If the circumstances involve other staff members, invite them to attend also. Be sure your note is dated, states the meeting's purpose, lists the names of others you've invited to attend, and suggests a definite time frame during which you might meet. For example, your note might read:

April 13, 2005

Dr. Monsman,

I need to meet with you sometime during the next week to discuss a problem regarding Marty Majors' grades in my classes and his eligibility for football this semester. Since Marty is our team's star quarterback, I've invited Coach Nelson to attend this meeting also.

Ms. Hystandard

c.c. Norm Nelson

A brief, detailed note, with copies sent to all interested parties (and one kept for your records), serves as documentation that you, in fact, requested a meeting with your administrator (and others) regarding your specific concern.

Once you make an appointment with your administrator, be sure to honor it. If unforeseen circumstances suddenly arise and you can't make the meeting, let the administrator know as soon as possible. Bring any materials to the meeting that might help your administrator gain a better understanding of the information you must convey. For example, if you must inform your principal that the school's star quarterback is failing in your class, and therefore is ineligible to play, bring a printed copy of the quarterback's grades; copies of all information given to him, his parents, and his coach regarding his need for academic improvement; documentation of your efforts to provide this student with additional help; and a large amount of courage.

Begin Positively and Empathetically

Begin by thanking your administrator for meeting with you. If appropriate to the situation and your administrator's persona, comment on some positive happenings in the school. You might say, for example, "Thank you for meeting with me Dr. Monsman. I know you've been very busy planning for this year's student achievement tests, and if the tests run as smoothly this year as last year, it'll be because of all of the extra planning you've done."

Positive comments must be factual and sincere, not fawning and disingenuous, and even though some administrators may appear to be unaffected by them, statements of encouragement do matter and are appreciated by almost all administrators regardless of their sophistication.

WARNING! AVOID COMPLIMENTING THIS ADMINISTRATOR

Almost all administrators appreciate receiving sincere and well-deserved compliments and do not take offense when their teachers offer them. However, there are a few administrators who view compliments from teachers with contempt. Generally speaking, these are people with highly authoritarian and rigid leadership styles who feel they must control their workers by maintaining an air of superiority over them. Therefore, they frown upon accepting compliments from those beneath them in the chain of command fearing, if they do, subordinates will view themselves as equals.

It's usually easy to identify administrators who view compassionate and supportive comments from their staff as complimentary power coups. For the most part, they run their schools in a highly formal and dictatorial fashion, associate only with those they perceive as on the same (or higher) leadership plane as themselves, and communicate with their teachers by fiat.

The easiest way to avoid alienating this type of administrator is to avoid complimenting them. However, if you are a hopeless optimist prone to complimenting others, voice only indirect and non-judgmental compliments to a compliment-eschewing administrator. Instead of saying, "I think you gave an excellent speech," which places you in the position of judging your administrator's speech-making abilities, you would say, "I really enjoyed your speech," which is a non-judgmental statement of fact.

Present Negative Information Diplomatically

Although your administrator may be aware of the meeting's purpose, sharing negative information still requires the use of good judgment. Avoid emotionally charged language and overstatement. Present information in a fair and reasoned fashion. Also, pass up the temptation to blame others for a problem you have created. You might say, "As you know, Dr. Monsman, I've asked to meet with you because there's a problem regarding Marty Major's eligibility to play in the state championship football game. Marty's grades are well below passing, and I believe I've done all that I can to help him improve them. I know the whole school will be disappointed if he doesn't play, but I also know that if an ineligible player participates in a game the team's entire season is subject to forfeit."

Address Questions and Concerns

When communicating bad news to your administrator, expect him or her to make inquiries and express concerns (usually in a most diplomatic fashion) to determine if you have done your job appropriately. For this reason, it is a good idea to bring with you any documentation you have regarding the meeting's topic. Depending on the circumstances and with your administrator's permission, it is also a good idea to invite those adults who can attest to your actions.

For example, as Marty Majors' teacher, you would bring Marty's work portfolio, copies of his graded tests, correspondence to his parents and coach informing them of his need for improvement, and a copy of the state athletic association's players' eligibility rules and guidelines.

Suggest Ways to Resolve Differences

Since you are dealing with your administrator, be prepared not only to suggest ways to resolve possible differences regarding the information you share, but also to accept any resolutions she may dictate. However, if you strongly disagree with the course of action dictated by your administrator, respectfully state your objection and make note of it in writing.

In Marty Majors' case, your administrator might suggest that you give Marty a "provisional passing grade" contingent upon his passing a comprehensive test to be administered *after* the state championship game. You oppose this solution and propose that Marty take the comprehensive test *before* the championship game.

Your administrator strongly disagrees with your proposal and dictates that you "pass this young man provisionally and administer the comprehensive test after the state championship has been won," whereupon you voice your dissent and follow your boss' dictate, but only after documenting your objections.

Communicating Unpleasant Information to Colleagues

Communicating unpleasant information to your colleagues differs from communicating unpleasant information to parents and administrators because you and your colleagues are professional equals. However, since you must work with and rely upon your colleagues on a daily basis, it is helpful to use tact when communicating unpleasant information to them.

Be Positive and Empathetic

Because you and your fellow teachers face many of the same job experiences, it's usually easy to begin positive and empathetic communications with them. Positive comments about well-behaved classes, well-planned lessons, and excellent rapport with students are always appreciated, as are commiserations about the challenges of dealing with over-crowded classes, lack of sufficient planning time, and ill-mannered students.

Present Negative Information Diplomatically

Most unpleasant information that you share with your teaching colleagues will involve complaints about them or their students. You can usually introduce your complaint by empathizing with the situation. If, for example, your complaint is about the excessive noise emanating from a colleague's classroom, you might introduce your concern by saying, "You really have a difficult group of students in your third-period class," or "I know it's really hard to get students to settle down right after physical education."

After your empathetic introduction, you can tactfully express your complaint, "Sometimes, even though the doors to my classroom are closed, the noise coming from your classroom makes it difficult for my students to concentrate."

When stating your concern, take care to refrain from overstatement and histrionics and avoid using hearsay to enhance your complaint. Don't say, for example, "I'm not the only one complaining. All the teachers at this end of the hall say something has to be done about the noise coming from your classroom!"

Address Questions and Concerns

If your complaint is about matters of classroom management and student discipline, your colleague is likely to question the course of action he or she could possibly take to improve matters. "I've tried to get that class to keep the noise down. They're all over the place. I just don't know what else to do with them."

You must then be prepared to offer some possible solutions. For example, you might suggest that your colleague rearrange the seating in the classroom to separate the talkers, plan less-interactive lessons for this particular class, or request an administrator observe the class to determine if some of the more difficult students would be better served by dividing them among several other classes.

PUT IT IN WRITING

Documentation is a critical, career-survival technique. In the case of Marty Majors, without documentation you could not substantiate the following: Marty is doing poorly in your class, you have made every effort to help him succeed, you have made his parents and coach aware of his poor performance, you are aware that Marty does not meet the eligibility requirements to play in the championship game, and you object to your administrator's directive allowing Marty to participate.

Therefore, it's essential to put things in writing since documentation can be used to:

- Verify you have fulfilled your job responsibilities.
- Confirm you have acted in a professional manner.
- Detail and substantiate your concerns.
- Provide information for self-analysis and personal improvement.
- Provide important information about the learning styles and behavior patterns of your students.
- Help you complete required tasks in a timely fashion.

When your complaint is about less-than-stellar work habits (for example, lateness for assigned duties, poor committee meeting attendance, or not following through adequately on team teaching projects), offending colleagues will question the accuracy of your statements. It is then up to you to provide documentation to substantiate your complaint.

Suggest Ways to Resolve Differences

If you and your colleague disagree on the seriousness of the problem or on how best to solve it, suggest some ways to resolve your differences. If you want her to show up each day for her assigned bus duty but she feels it's unnecessary because "there are more people assigned to bus duty than they really need," you might suggest that she get others to do her coverage for her or that she speak with the administration and get them to assign her to another non-teaching duty or reduce the number of teachers assigned to bus duty. You might also remind her that she can be held legally liable if a student is injured in her area of coverage when she is not there.

Communicating in Less-Than-Ideal Circumstances

In the ideal world, all schools have supportive environments where effective communication always takes place. In reality, however, many schools have impersonal, cynical, or fearful environments where effective communication is difficult, and sometimes nearly impossible. Only a strong, positive attitude, sheer intractable determination, and a fervent desire to do a good job can help a teacher exist in such environments; yet, if you find yourself in one of these situations, it is helpful to understand some of the negative dynamics that take place and to have some practical strategies for communicating your compliments, concerns, complaints, and questions more effectively.

Communicating in Impersonal Learning Environments

Impersonal learning environments are usually found in large secondary schools with diverse student populations, many teachers, a variety of support personnel, and numerous administrators. Without strong and caring leadership, large schools can easily develop an atmosphere of coldly detached self-interest in which students become hedonistic, teachers teach in a perfunctory fashion, and administrators approach problems impassively. As a result, the quality of education declines.

The best way to make an impersonal learning environment more hospitable is to try to personalize your communication whenever possible. While this may not change the tenor of an entire school, it will have a positive effect on those around you and make your classroom a better place in which to learn.

Here are some strategies that can help you communicate effectively on a more personal level:

- Learn the names of everyone you have dealings with and use their names when speaking with them.

- Strive to make a set number of positive personal comments during each class. For example, if your set number of positive personal comments is three per class, during one class you might make a positive remark about one student's new hair style, another's performance in a school play, and a third's kindness to another classmate.

- Whenever possible, attend your students' sporting events, plays, musical performances, and other extracurricular activites.

- Write brief, positive, personalized comments on student-written work that you grade. You might write, for example, "Great idea, Jessica," "A novel approach to problem solving, Rico," or "Chris, you definitely have your own style."

- Send at least two (or whatever number you can easily manage) positive notes or emails to different parents each week. For example:

Dear Mr. & Mrs. Olsen,

Just wanted you to know that the twins are doing an outstanding job in drama class.

Sincerely,

Personalized Teacher

Communicating in Cynical Environments

Cynical environments exist in schools on all levels. They often develop when a school's student demographics change over a period of years but most of the original teachers remain. These teachers, feeling they are holding their students to high standards, refuse to modify their teaching to meet their students' needs. Because the students cannot meet the success expected of them, they soon become disinterested and disrespectful, making the teachers frustrated, bitter, and cynical. If you are an optimistic and dedicated teacher surrounded by cynical colleagues, it's often difficult not to become cynical yourself. One way to avoid becoming overly negative is always to communicate in an upbeat, positive, and responsible fashion. The following strategies, applied with finesse, good humor, and determination, can help you manage such communications.

- Politely refuse to participate in negative conversations about students, parents, colleagues, or administrators.

- Avoid making soapbox speeches to cynical colleagues informing them of the errors of their ways.

- When a colleague makes a cynical remark, rephrase it in more positive terms, and then, if possible, refute it. For example,

    Cynic: That Tori Lyles is the dimmest bulb in the package. I think if you looked in one of that kid's ears, you could see right through to the other side.

    You: Well, we all have our strengths and weaknesses, Mr. C, and Tori's actually doing pretty well in my science class this semester.

- Refute a colleague's cynical comment with a "yes but" positive comment of your own. For example,

    Cynic: Oh brother, we have a faculty meeting this afternoon. What a waste of time!

You: Yeah, looks like there's one scheduled, but we haven't had a faculty meeting for some time now and I'm kind of anxious to get some information about the new tests we're supposed to administer later this year.

Communicating in Fearful Environments

Schools can have overtly fearful environments or subtly fearful environments. Overtly fearful environments are those in which students and staff members actually live in fear of physical harm, while in subtly fearful environments, students and staff members live in fear of failure and ridicule.

Schools with overtly fearful environments are dangerous and chaotic places, instilling fear in people in some way. These schools often need intervention from law enforcement officials, government agencies, and community activists in order to regain control and change their unhealthy dynamics. Little in the way of education can take place in such schools until they undergo significant restructuring.

Unfortunately, though they are few and far between, such unsafe schools do exist. If you are assigned to teach in a school with an overtly fearful environment, the following communication strategies along with a strong behavior management plan and plenty of fortitude may prove helpful.

In overtly fearful enviornments you should:

- Seek assistance from other staff members or the administration, rather than place yourself in danger by single-handedly confronting large groups of disruptive students whom you do not know.

- Stay calm, avoid raising your voice, and speak assertively when communicating with difficult students.

- Separate troublemakers from a group and speak with them individually whenever possible.

- Avoid using expletives, racial slurs, and other derogatory comments regardless of how freely your students may use them.

- Always try to teach well-planned lessons and make every attempt to model appropriate behavior regardless of how futile it may seem.

Subtly fearful schools have dogmatic and repressive environments often created by district supervisors or administrators who employ a "my way or the highway" philosophy in order to "keep everyone on the same page and moving in the right direction." These schools are run in a very formal and excessively organized fashion. Every activity must take place according to schedule, lessons may not deviate from "the norm," and classrooms that emanate noise are perceived as "out of control" and in need of "administrative assistance."

Because the teachers working in these micromanaged places feel pressure to control everything and everyone, they are less patient and more punitive with their students. The students then become anxious at best and defiant at worst. Therefore, in subtly fearful schools, little in the way of creative, interactive, and enjoyable education takes place since students live in fear of their teachers, teachers live in fear of their administrators, and administrators live in fear of their supervisors.

In subtly fearful enviornments you should:

- Express your student expectations in gently positive rather than bluntly negative terms. For example, the blunt, "No talking in class," might be stated more gently as, "Be considerate of others and do not speak when they are speaking." The negatively threatening, "Lateness to class will be punished by detention," could be replaced with, "Students are expected to be in class on time."

- Praise your students as often as possible. While this may seem like an obvious and automatic teaching strategy, those who teach in subtly fearful schools for extended periods of time soon believe it is unnecessary to praise students for something they are supposed to be doing anyway.

- Engage your students in positive and pleasant (yet well-controlled) learning activities.

- Plan lessons that give your students less structure and more movement. For example, plan class plays, lessons outside or in the gym, field trips, and such.

Communicating effectively in a subtly fearful environment can be difficult, especially if you wish to convey a slightly less-intimidating message than is normally conveyed at your school. You must take care to avoid communicating an "us versus them" message to your students and to enforce the rules followed by everyone else in your school. However, within the bounds of those rules, you can strive to make the atmosphere in your classroom more student-friendly and less stressful by employing these strategies.

Appendix

Interpreting Non-Verbal Communication

People communicate their thoughts, feelings, and attitudes in many different ways, and not all of them are direct or intentional. Sometimes they reveal their true feelings through unconscious mannerisms or contradictions between their demeanor and professional status. The purpose of the following charts is not to have you make rash judgments about yourself or others, but rather to help you develop an awareness of some unintended messages you might convey to others, as well as some that they might convey to you.

Body Language and Its Meanings	
Action	**Possible Meanings**
Standing or sitting very erect, arms crossed over one's chest or stiff at one's side	Rigid, unfriendly, unwelcoming, no-nonsense, closed off, cold
Sitting slumped or slouched down in chair	Apathetic, careless, overly familiar, disrespectful, tired
Sitting, arms crossed, legs crossed tightly, facing away from speaker	Resentful, uncomfortable, closed off, angry, upset
Staying further away from the speaker than necessary for personal space, avoiding or shrugging off innocuous touch	Distrustful, angry, fearful, phobia of small spaces
Avoiding eye contact or viewing the speaker from the corner of one's eye	Suspicious, nervous, annoyed, shy
Standing within inches of someone, inside their personal space	Socially inept, overly forceful, making sexual advance
Touching someone excessively, beyond what is acceptable for level of acquaintance	Socially inept, sexual advance
Hanging back during introduction, rejecting handshakes, poor eye contact	Excessively shy, unfriendly, socially inept
Good eye contact, relaxed demeanor, paying attention to all, ready smile	Friendly, competent, socially aware, accepting, approachable

Detrimental Behaviors and the Messages They Convey	
Behavior/Characteristic	Message
Making faces (grimacing, rolling eyes, sneering)	Judgmental, immature, disrespectful
"Copping an attitude," surly	Keep away, overly aggressive
Prankishness	Immature, covertly aggressive
Avoiding responsibility	Self-indulgent, indolent, apathetic, fearful
Arrogant, know-it-all	Sense of superiority, unwillingness to accept help
Excessively solicitous to authority figures	Untrustworthy, fearful, cowardly
Excessively possessive of school-provided equipment and materials ("My classroom, my books, my overhead, my computer")	Self-centered, overly controlling
Rumor-mongering	Untrustworthy
Self-righteous	Arrogant, unaccepting

Style of Dress and the Negative Messages It Can Convey	
Style of Dress	**Possible Negative Message**
Provocative, tight fitting, revealing	Extreme sexuality, narcissistic
Inappropriate for setting (cocktail dress for sporting event)	Socially inept, attention seeking
Stylistically extreme (goth, hip-hop)	Immature, rebellious
Excessive body ornamentation (tattoos, body piercings, radical hair coloring or make-up)	Attention seeking, rebellious, immature
Dirty clothing, uncombed hair, poor personal hygiene	Poor self-concept, economically deprived, rebellious
Clothing that is markedly avant-garde	Attention seeking
Clothing that is out-of-date or totally devoid of fashion awareness	Self-absorbed